Astrology
Interpreted

Astrology Interpreted

Your complete guide to the stars

by Charlotte Abell Walker

Hubbard Press

Northbrook, Illinois 60062

Cover:

Paper Sculpture: Edward Boehmer
Photograph: Michael Mauney

Contents

Contents

Contents

Contents

Under a Lucky Star

Were You Born Under a Lucky Star?

Those who have succeeded best in life have had the good fortune to adopt the calling for which they were best fitted. This is generally the result of what is called chance, that convenient scapegoat on which we place our good or ill luck, and frequently hold responsible for our incapacity.

How few successes we meet, how many failures we pass on our journey through life!

To tell what occupation to adopt, and what line of life to follow, what associates and partners to choose, how to recognize the possibilities and limitations of our friends and ourselves, is the purpose of this book.

Occupation
Associates
Partners

It deals with the other important subjects— marriage and the education of children.

Marriage
Children

What is said here is not new; it is the wisdom of ages culled from the minds of ancient and modern philosophers.

When we speak of the influence of the stars on the life of a man or woman, many, who consider themselves wise and learned, smile with a look of pitying condescension and brush aside all belief in such "nonsense" with a sarcastic or angry denial.

One of the easiest ways to obtain a transitory reputation for wisdom is to ridicule and deny what one does not understand.

" Error runs down an inclined plane, while Truth has to laboriously climb its way up hill."

Individual liberty

Another avowed object of this book is to plead for individual liberty. We hear so often and with so much impatience the expression, " I would not do so and so, if I were you," that it seems high time to look for the real cause of why our way seems better to us than that of another, for, as Locke says, " We are seldom at ease from the solicitations of our natural or adopted desires."

Heredity

The problem of heredity, to which we have paid much attention of late, gives us only half an answer to our question, and close investigation reveals to us the fact that there are other forces back of heredity which cannot be ignored, but must be taken into consideration when we seek to find the true reason for the likeness and yet great unlikeness of children born of the same parents. The theory of heredity is only one side of the problem we are to solve, in the study of the individuality of every human being; if it comprised the whole, then clever parents would always produce clever children, and stupid ones would bring forth dullards, but we know that often just the contrary conditions exist.

The author has no intention of going deeply into an investigation of all the forces which go to make an individual just *himself* and no other, but only to present another phase of the subject to be studied, in connection with the problems of heredity—this is the effect of planetary influence on human life. If an investigation of this subject will furnish us with a clew to unravel the mysteries of self, and help us to find our proper place in the world, help us to select the life-work we are best adapted to, then it is a proper and profitable study for all mankind.

Success depends upon the work being suited to the worker, and the chief lesson for us to learn is to recognize our limitations and work within the scope of our ability. Our inclinations may be pleasanter to follow, but they are not so profitable, and a wise person will endeavor to distinguish between the two, and choose that which will be for his ultimate good.

Know thyself

Vocation

In that portion of this book devoted to vocation, the aptness of each type for the work they are best calculated to do is only suggested, but the suggestions offered may prove helpful to those who flounder in a sea of uncertainty. Long before the necessity for real work arises, aptness for certain kinds of work manifests itself, not so plainly to the future worker as to the student of human nature. Children show the bent of their minds not at study, but when following their own inclinations and at play; it is then that they should be watched, and peculiar characteristics noted for future use.

Our success in life, then, depends upon a thorough understanding of our capabilities. We have certain innate faculties, as our aspirations plainly demonstrate, and these should be developed, and carefully exercised. The raw material lies in our hands to do with as we will, but we must *will* to do that which some indwelling, never-to-be-suppressed longing tells us that we possess, and which seeks to find outward expression in our life-work. But we are lazy thinkers, as a rule, and prefer to have our questions decided for us, and we meekly suppress our intuition and reason, in

Innate faculties

Individuality

12

deference to those who coolly assert the supremacy of their minds over our own, and instead of developing our talents along lines laid down for us by the Creator, we become weak imitators. Then, when great moments arise, and we are called upon to produce our best, not the reflection of some one else's best, we suddenly discover that we have not lived our own lives, have not done our own work, and that failure is the only result. That which we can do best, no other can do for us. Another's talents may be greater, but they belong to him, and can never be ours; we must cultivate our own talents in our own way, for, as Spencer so aptly remarks, " A man may turn which way he will, he may undertake no matter what, but he will find himself at last compelled to move along the track nature has marked out for him."

Aptitude

The hidden laws of nature are as an open book to the earnest searcher. " Seek and ye shall find," investigate before denying, are two injunctions which he never disregards. The truth of a statement may be denied by an ignoramus, but it takes a wise man, or one who has some knowledge of the subject, to contradict it.

Persons who have formed the lazy habit of denying, instead of investigating, may regard, as foolish superstition, the ideas put forth in this book, and pronounce them unworthy of serious consideration. To such persons we can only say that, " nothing makes a mind so imprudent and so bold as ignorance of past times and old books."

Claudius Ptolemy, the earliest known writer on the subject of astrology, and from whom all later writers have drawn their information, says that he bases his deductions on, " the rules of the ancients whose observations were founded in nature." Another writer informs us that, " no attempt has ever been made by either ancient or modern writers to explain the figures of the signs of the Zodiac or assign an inventor to them."

This alleged superstition has numbered among its believers, not only the learned men of all countries far back into the remote ages, but also our Jewish patriarchs down to, " the wise men," whose knowledge of the science of the stars foretold the exact time of the birth of the Christ. Astronomy and mathematics owe their origin to astrology, which is a vast storehouse of truths taught to men in the world's infancy by the " sons of God " when they came down to earth, and walked and talked with men.

That this science has fallen into disrepute,

Investigate

Ptolemy

Biblical testimony

14

owing to the fact that some of its secrets were laid hold of by unworthy hands, is not to be denied; but it must have had the strong foundation of truth to have withstood the assault of those who have either honestly, maliciously, or ignorantly assailed it.

Twelve Types of People

The wise men of old tell us that there are twelve distinct types of people in the world who have their special place and work to do in the plan of the universe, and that they can be classified under their appropriate sign of the Zodiac.

The writer of this book has been for years faithful and persistent in the study of this half-forgotten lore, has carefully investigated biographies of well-known men and women, studied and compared the general characteristics of friends and relatives, and only asks that the reader will not condemn the assertions made herein until he has also, by personal observation and comparison, given the subject thoughtful consideration.

Forgotten lore

In studying the influence of the planets, we find that persons born at about the same time of a month are alike in their general characteristics, but we find also that education, circumstances, and environment all have a modifying effect, and that other planets may work either for or against them.

The belief that at times planets have a malefic effect on our lives finds confirmation in the Scriptures, when we examine critically the many allusions made to the influence of the heavenly orbs. When Deborah said, " The stars in their courses fought against Sisera," is it not reasonable to suppose that she referred to certain well-known astrological statements ? For instance, in casting a horoscope, the easternmost star is the strongest, and as long as it is above the horizon the fortune of the person for whom the horoscope is cast is said to be in the ascendant.

Planetary influence

Now, while it is claimed that persons born at about the same time of a month are alike in character, it does not necessarily follow that they will seem alike to a superficial observer; but if one will test the correctness of this statement by classifying himself and friends under their appropriate signs, he will find that in fundamental characteristics they are essentially the same, although one may be conquered by, and another have conquered, the faults of his or her sign.

16

The Cusp

The discriminating judgment of the reader must be exercised still further. The length of a sign is about thirty days. The sun passes successively through the twelve signs during a year, but it will be noticed that he enters a sign about the twentieth of the month; technically speaking, it requires six days in a sign to constitute a residence, therefore a person born between the first and seventh days of a sign, is said to be on the cusp, and *partakes of some of the characteristics of the preceding sign.* This fact, taken into consideration with the adverse influence of other planets, at the time of birth, accounts for the contradictory traits of character often found in a person who has not learned to harmonize the warring elements in his own nature, and also the difference between persons born under the same sign. As an instance of this fact, Mr. Andrew Carnegie was born on the cusp of Sagittarius (November 25th). The author, who has studied his character only through the means of newspapers and biographical sketches, would, from the knowledge thus gleaned, unhesitatingly classify him under Scorpio, and having very few if any of the traits of the Sagittarius character; while Mr. Henry C. Frick, born

Contradictions explained

17

December 19th, is fully under the influence of the latter sign.

Shortcomings

In calling attention to the faults of a sign, it should be borne in mind that, " we should not speak of our own or others' faults—at least not openly—unless to some useful purpose." It has not been the author's intention to provide a scourge with which we may lash our friends, but to call attention to the faults and tendencies of one's own sign.

Self-knowledge is man's greatest inheritance, and until he has the power to face his own soul, he will never be able to conquer his limitations.

We are all too ready to call attention to the work others should do, and neglect our own, and in choosing words to express our thoughts we give little heed to the sorrow they may unnecessarily cause sensitive hearts. Words are things, and these living messengers, " speed o'er the track to bring you back, whatever went out from your mind."

It would be well for highly-strung, passionate natures to note the effect on themselves of their frequent outbursts of temper. They

Critical of others

18

would soon discover that they had thrown out an evil force which reacted on themselves in the form of headache, disordered nerves, and inability to proceed with their own work, until their passion had subsided. To do each day our own work *well* is all our duty; to give way to anger, jealousy, or grumbling, because another's lot is cast in pleasanter places than our own, is only a form of self-indulgence almost as bad in its effect on ourselves as the greater vice of intemperance. But the faults and vices of human nature become steps in the ladder of character building one by one, as they are surmounted.

Reaction

Affinities and Marriage

What is said on the subject of partners applies in a measure to marriage and choice of associates.

If we find that our life is linked, either by birth or from choice, with those who are not harmonious to us, would it not be wiser to seek the cause of the discord, and if not possible to remove it, to avoid at least playing on the discordant string?

Harmonious

However, an understanding of self and the *desire* as well as the ability to blend our differ-

19

Companionship

ing characteristics with others, is the only safe guide to follow in the search for true companionship. We should like our friends for what they *are*, not for what we would make them. The world would be a very stupid place to live in if we were all modelled on the same pattern.

Let us strive to respect individuality in others as we would have our own respected, and, "agree to differ but never to disagree." If our friends have faults, so have we, and it can be called little else than egotism to point out weaknesses in others, until we have conquered our own.

Egotism

Suggestions to Parents and Teachers

Purpose

In offering suggestions to parents and teachers, the purpose is to indicate, not in detail, but in general, that which concerns the real development and education of a child for its permanent good.

Unfortunately, no preparation whatever is considered necessary for the important position of parenthood, and the chief qualification of a teacher is to be able to pass certain intellectual examinations; questions as to real fitness for this work are seldom asked.

While a blooded animal's characteristics are carefully considered and trained in the right direction, children of a large family are in most instances brought up by one method. Many children suffer great nervous irritation from the habit of considering them collectively, instead of individually; from the terrible lack of sympathy existing between them and those who have undertaken their moral and intellectual guidance.

It is impossible to give any real, permanent, or intelligent help to children so long as those in authority over them persist in thinking that, "all the virtues are with the rulers and the vices with the ruled."

Self-mastery

Self-mastery is the most important lesson for a true educator to learn. He must recognize his own faults and conquer them before he is prepared to fill this high office, for when one does not know his own imperfections and limitations, he unconsciously places many obstacles in his own pathway.

The method of discipline pursued by parents and teachers who have not learned self-control, is to vent their displeasure on these small offenders in sharp words or rough shakings. Such correction is harmful to the child, and diminishes his respect for the person who makes such an exhibition of ill-temper; nor

Methods of discipline

is such a one careful to distinguish between a trait of character which is really a fault and a mannerism that does not meet with his or her approval.

Demanding instant and unquestioning obedience is also harmful, as coercive restraint tends to weaken character. Children who are brought up in this manner are apt to regard their parents as sort of friend-enemies, who are constantly thwarting their desires and cravings for experience, without inquiring as to whether their motives are good or bad. This method weakens and finally breaks that bond of sympathy between them which is so essential to all wise control.

A child shows the desire to exercise its own reasoning faculties by constantly asking, " Why ? " in its attempt to find the balance between the true and the false. The answer, " Because I told you so," may silence, but Education never satisfies. It is a deplorable fact that this manner of education is the chief cause of so many bright children developing into weak, imitative, conventional, unprogressive men and women.

The right to think for themselves is denied them, because they are considered incompetent to exercise any judgment, and no effort is made to help them become self-governing individuals. On the contrary, the supreme purpose of parental control seems to be the subjugation of the child's will and the restriction of its supposed depravity.

If our children were to have no more independence when they reach adulthood than was accorded them under the old Roman law, when the power of the *patria potestas* was absolute even over the life of his son, whom he might alienate or destroy without accounting to any earthly tribunal, there might be some wisdom in not permitting them to exercise their own will power, and accustoming them to submit without a murmur to the control of another. But as they are some day to become self-directing men and women, it would seem better judgment to aid them to gain self-reliance while still under the parental roof and watchful eyes of those who should have their real interest at heart.

Responding to the motives of others does not cultivate a spirit of self-reliance; allowing the thoughts of others to dominate us, lessens our power for original thinking. The chief elements in a child's life are love of liberty and productive activity. In order to give them real help we must aid them to harmonize submission and liberty, to substitute coöperation for obstinacy, and independence for subserviency.

Patria potestas

Harmonize

23

Teachers should not try to dominate the interest of children, but should endeavor to arouse their self-active interest, which is the only persistent, propelling motive to any effort; then there will no longer be any complaint that children are not interested in their work. So long as the present system of discipline is pursued, it would be more accurate to say that the children are not interested in the teacher's work.

Duties of parents

The obstacles children have to overcome are stupendous. In every-day business matters we seek to find the lines of least resistance, and when discovered try to work with and not against them. Short-sighted parents make no such effort, and are apt to presume that their children's needs are similar to their own, instead of realizing that each child has its own individuality to develop, and that it is the duty of parents to help it unlock its own powers. So long as they continue to force the proverbial square child into the round hole, they will continue to spoil a good farmer, mechanic, or artist, and produce, possibly, a poor lawyer, physician, or business man. This forcing process, seen in every-day life, shows how the real ability of children is misapprehended and disregarded.

All this consideration of individual traits

24

means increased responsibility, and may neces-   Responsibility
sitate many changes in our conduct generally
towards the young.   It will force us to make
our motives higher, our lives purer and broader,
and give us a better conception of our duties;
then we will become able to develop the higher,
finer faculties in children with an ease which
will startle us.

The various works consulted in the preparation of this book are: Ptolemy's " Tetra-
biblos, or Quadripartite "; " The Primum
Mobile," by Placidus; Lilly's " Astrology,"
Sibley's " Astrology," " Mysteries of Astrology," Wilson's " Dictionary of Astrology,"
" Theoretical Basis of Astrology," " Kabalis-
tic Astrology," " Mazzaroth," " The Secret
Doctrine," and many others on the subjects
of astrology, psychology, and education.

CAPRICORN

The Goat

Planet

ℏ

Saturn

General Characteristics

The most noticeable feature of persons born under this sign is their desire for intellectual attainments. They are proud, self-reliant, and very practical; but they are also great idealists and place their standard of excellence unreasonably high—in fact, they are so fastidious that they are seldom satisfied with anything short of perfection. They adore the beautiful in art and nature. Even though they are excellent financial managers and seldom fail to make both ends meet, it is very difficult for them to economize in small matters, their personal tastes are so luxurious.

Intellectual

Luxurious
tastes

In manner Capricorn people are cool, calm, and collected; they are not fond of demonstration except from those they really love, but they lose heart when well-merited praise is withheld or their efforts are not appreciated. In matters of love or friendship they seem to be fickle, but they are really very faithful and sincere; they care for but few, and are prone to endow the objects of their affection with every good and noble attribute; this habit causes them much unhappiness, for their ideals are seldom realized.

Although Capricorn people are naturally industrious, they are not willing servers of others. In carrying out their own plans they will work with unflagging zeal and determination to surmount every obstacle which stands between them and success. They seldom seek advice or protection from others, and while fate seems against them, as a rule, they bear their burdens with much fortitude; their great patience, perseverance, and industry enable them to endure many hardships, and they frequently conquer adverse circumstances and environment by sheer force of mental grip. When these people are thoroughly interested in an undertaking, in espousing an unpopular cause, or in pushing to victory a forlorn hope, all the combativeness in their nature is aroused; it is always a battle of brains for Capricorn people. They are better organizers than fighters, they conquer because of their quickness to take advantage of the weak points in the opposing forces, and their refusal to contemplate even the possibility of defeat.

They hold very stubbornly to their ideas of right and wrong, resent any interference in affairs of their own, and never pry into the

Industrious

Persistent

affairs of others. They have a high moral nature and great regard for duty; are inclined to stick rather closely to public opinion, except in matters of religious belief; on this subject they reserve the right to do their own thinking, and seldom accept any statement that cannot be logically demonstrated. In literature they prefer the philosophic and scientific; they are public spirited, and have a natural taste for politics; their commercial instinct is large, and they are the natural organizers of great enterprises.

In general conversation they are bright, subtle, and witty, but when opposed in an argument they become unyielding, and assert their views in a very harsh and positive manner. When Capricorn people succeed in overcoming the self-consciousness which often makes them appear awkward and constrained, they have an ease and freedom of manner which establishes at once a feeling of friendship and wins for them many friends. They are endowed with excellent memories, are good story-tellers and deep thinkers; they love solitude, and often have spells of great despondency which seem utterly without reason until one understands the influence of Saturn in this sign.

High moral nature

Subtle

Deep thinkers

Capricorn

SHORTCOMINGS

Capricorn people are abnormally sensitive and self-conscious; this causes them to be ever on the lookout for slights. They seldom retaliate even when they have been deeply wronged, but grow cold and hard, because while they forgive, they never forget, and when deceived in a friend they sometimes lose health and all interest in life, become indifferent to the society of others, and give themselves up to a life of gloomy meditation and solitude. They are usually victims of overwork, and become so selfishly absorbed in their own duties that they ignore the claims of others until they have completed their self-appointed task. When their attention is called to this trait in their character, which should be called selfishness, though sometimes termed intensity, they keenly feel the rebuke, become very despondent, and plead their inability to work in any other way. When Capricorn people are reckless in their expenditures or are overtaken by misfortune, like the goat, the emblem of their sign, they will make the most of their surroundings, and subsist on next to nothing, with an air of sturdy self-reliance which admits of no patronizing.

Sensitive

Selfish

SUGGESTIONS

Capricorn people should restrain their tendency to go to extremes. As they ruin their best powers by too close adherence to duty, they should be less prodigal of their strength, and work with more discrimination, if they would avoid the usual physical and nervous prostration which follows their efforts. Persistency and steadiness are fine attributes, but as evil is only good inverted, these two qualities may degenerate into obstinacy and unchangeableness. "The sin of finishing" is sometimes as much to be deplored as neglect of duty. These people should seek to cultivate a good "forgettery" as being, in their case, much more desirable than a good memory. Give up the habit of introspection and care less for the opinion and approbation of others.

Renounce introspection

When placed in positions of authority, they should strive to subdue any tendency towards haughtiness or arrogance in dealing with others, and bear in mind the fact that a fine organizer and manager is not a despot who rules by force, but one who directs and governs because his methods bring about the best results.

The mission of Capricorn people is to overcome obstacles; to conquer, and not to be conquered by, their limitations; to do this they must look up and away from self, take account of their weaknesses, not to deplore, as is their habit, but to overcome them.

Affinities and Marriage

Those who look for a soft, yielding disposition will not find it in the Capricorn nature. The women of this sign, while they make loving and devoted wives, are firm and positive in their opinions, and find the domestic life, as a rule, too narrow for their ability; they are seldom happy in the married life, unless united with those who respect individuality of character in others. They demand justice and appreciation rather than outward demonstrations of affection. These people care for but few, and of them they are very jealous, and will brook no rivals even in ordinary friendships.

Attractions   They are naturally attracted to those born under Taurus and Virgo, but their most congenial matrimonial alliances are made with those born under Cancer, Sagittarius, or Aquarius. Capricorn and Aries seldom agree long at a time, and a union with one born under Scorpio is not advisable, because the tendency of persons born under the latter sign is to arbitrarily rule others, and it is almost impossible for a true Capricorn nature to submit to dictation.

Suggestions to Parents and Teachers

Capricorn children from their inherent managing ability are apt to assume a haughty, arrogant manner when giving directions to playmates and servants. This habit should be checked at once, and their attention called, not only to the poor service rendered under coercion, but also to their own resentfulness when spoken to in a peremptory tone. These children, while naturally industrious, are not willing servers of others, and require to be taught that service does not necessarily mean servitude, and that voluntary service implies perfect freedom. When they fully comprehend this lesson, they become very helpful and efficient, but they should be allowed to do their own planning, as much as possible, and when their work is well done, praise should be given unstintedly. They need a great deal of encouragement to arouse their dormant ambition, for the tendency of persons born under

Check arrogance

Inculcate voluntary service

this sign is to make the most of their present situation. When Capricorn people have not received a good education they are usually content all through life to do manual work for a moderate remuneration. As they belong mainly to the commercial world, every Capricorn child should receive a practical business education, and have some real experience in self-maintenance, even if there is no other object in view than the development of character.

Educate practically

No greater mistake can be made in the management of Capricorn children than to ridicule or speak sarcastically of their apparent lack of ambition, for they are very sensitive, and really are deficient in self-esteem, despite their habit of self-assertion, and to call them slow or stupid is to make them so.

Severe criticism harmful

Sarcasm is a luxury to indulge in with equals, but never with children or inferiors, for in the latter case it has only the effect of drawing out an impertinent retort, and causes a sensitive child to lose heart and discourages him in the effort to please.

When Capricorn children lack continuity, it is because their interest, through faulty management, has not been fully awakened; they love to work, and when given a task, with a certain amount of responsibility attached, they will work untiringly to overcome difficulties, if

Impose responsibility

only to prove themselves worthy of the trust reposed in them. These children are natural students; patient and persevering, as can be easily discerned by watching them when following their own inclinations at work or play.

Fortunately for our future men and women, the age has passed when parents and teachers fancied a child's mind could be made to order. We are beginning to realize the importance of developing and aiding the growth of individuality, and are becoming wise enough to make our methods of training subservient to the spontaneous unfolding of these young minds in their progress towards maturity.

Women

VOCATION

The women born under this sign are excellent housekeepers and discreet financial managers. They are faithful and devoted in their domestic relations, not demonstrative, but very sincere and loyal to those they love. They are usually considered cold and unfeeling, but they are not really so. They are abnormally sensitive and self-conscious, but lack self-esteem; this causes them to conceal their intense and ardent nature, under a crust of icy reserve

Loyal

35

which is very hard to break through, but when they feel that they are really liked, and their motives understood, they become genial and affectionate.

Patient

When they are not afflicted with disordered nerves, caused by overwork and worrying over trifles, they are very kind-hearted and patient, even under the most trying circumstances. They are very self-reliant, and do not like to be interfered with in their methods of managing their household or their work; they will listen to suggestions from others, but will not adopt them until carefully considered and compared with their own ideas.

Natural planners

They are natural planners, very neat and orderly, have fine taste in dress and in the arrangement of their homes. They are hospitably inclined and are excellent entertainers, but they are subject to spells of depression from which it is difficult to arouse them, and at such times seem to lose all interest in life. These gloomy spells are caused by the influence of the planet Saturn; indeed, it is a rare thing to find a person born under this sign who is not subject to fits of despondency without any apparent cause.

Despondent

As teachers Capricorn women have marked ability and a genuine love for the work; they seek to arouse the child's self-active interest, and their method of discipline is an appeal to its sense of honor. Many fine writers, actresses, and dramatic readers are born under this sign. The real genius and indomitable perseverance of a Capricorn woman is rarely ever developed until she is thrown on her own resources or occupies a position of responsibility.

Literary and dramatic ability

Some of the well-known women born under this sign are: Lucretia Mott, Olga Nethersole, Maria Edgeworth, Myra Clark Gaines, Mrs. John Drew (the elder), Mrs. Chapman Catt, and Laura Bridgman.

Distinguished women

Men

VOCATION

Capricorn men belong mainly to the commercial world. They are quick as lightning to grasp an opportunity, and never fail to see the money-making side of a scheme. They have great foresight, and are excellent judges of character. They are singularly capable as managers of large enterprises, for they have the unusual ability to both plan and execute. It is a mistake, however, for a Capricorn man, when he occupies a position of authority, to give too much attention to detail work, and

Executive and managing ability

thus limit the scope of his executive force and power to wield a controlling influence over others. For this detail work he should select employees born under Pisces and Taurus, for these people are natural servers of others and are very faithful in carrying out instructions. Should he have one of his own type in his employ, he should simply indicate the work to be done, and leave the method of execution to such employee, who will never manifest his real ability until definite responsibility rests upon him, and who, if he is constantly interfered with and directed as to methods, will not render his best service, and will likely become discouraged and resentful when thus ignorantly oppressed.

Hotel managers

Capricorn men are also very efficient in taking charge of large institutions or hotels; they show great tact and patience in their management of servants, and while they prefer to direct others, they are not above doing the manual work, when such necessity arises, and are seldom thrown into confusion at the loss of a trusted employee.

Military and naval commanders

In politics and public life they are positive, even dogmatic in their opinions, and stand out strongly for party interests. Some Capricorn men are found among the successful military and naval commanders, but their success is due to their managing ability, rather than to any fighting element in their nature.

Many fine writers, novelists, and statesmen are born under this sign. In the legal profession they are fine reasoners, and spend much time on the elaboration of their briefs, no detail being too trifling to escape their attention. As actors and orators they have considerable personal magnetism; this is especially true of those who are born on the Cusp. Some musicians and artists come under this sign, but, as a rule, the practical side of the Capricorn nature is stronger than the artistic, and they naturally turn their attention to such lines of work as require sound judgment and painstaking, systematic management. They are good financiers and can usually devise a way to make both ends meet.

Legal ability

Good financiers

PARTNERSHIPS

A partnership formed between Capricorn and Sagittarius, if both were fitted by education to fill high positions in the business world, should enable them to become a great commercial and money-making firm; their combined sagacity would bring about splendid results. Capricorn should leave the detail work to Sagittarius, and attend principally to the plans for their commercial interests.

Capricorn and Aquarius would work harmoniously together, but they would not soar quite so high in their financial schemes because of the lack of positiveness in the character of the Aquarius man. Taurus and Virgo would coöperate successfully with the Capricorn nature. While the pleasantest business relations would exist between Capricorn and Cancer, the conservatism of the latter would have a tendency to thwart the best efforts of the former.

Distinguished men

The distinguished men born under this sign are: Daniel Webster, Charles Sumner, William E. Gladstone, Disraeli, Edmund Burke, Alma Tadema, Rudyard Kipling, Admiral George Dewey, General Joubert, Irving M. Scott, and Thomas Alexander Scott.

Planetary Influence

MENTAL

Saturn's influence in this sign is very hard to overcome. Persons born under his rays usually meet with much opposition, and climb the ladder of success with difficulty. He governs the reflective faculties and produces studious, scientific, and close reasoners; he steadies and strengthens the mentality, makes the manner harsh and severe, gives intense love of justice, business sagacity, economy, and persistence.

MORAL

The malign influences of this planet can be overcome by Capricorn people conquering their suspicious, discontented natures. They must realize that materialism and love of external things is their ruin and look beyond the limitations of self. Planetary influence on human life is downward, and if it seeks to find expression through the animal senses, such influence must be overcome to insure true progress in any direction.

PHYSICAL

On the physical plane Saturn gives a medium stature, dark eyes, brownish hair, and sallow complexion. Persons who are well under his influence have large foreheads, with reason and ideality well developed. The action of Saturn on the health is always slow and insidious; he undermines the vitality, governs chronic disorders, and causes melancholia, indigestion, nervous prostration, and rheumatism. His most potent influence is felt every seventh year.

The white onyx, sometimes called chalcedony, is supposed to possess mystical power when worn by a native of Capricorn.

AQUARIUS

January 20
to
February 19

The Waterman

Planets

♄   ♂

Saturn   Uranus

General Characteristics

Persons born under this sign are naturally endowed with great possibilities, but they usually require a strong incentive to force them into action. When great occasions arise and they become thoroughly aroused, they show wonderful strength of purpose, and when they feel convinced that the stand they have taken or the methods they have adopted are correct, no amount of reasoning or persuasion will induce them to change. They are earnest students of human nature, and are not easily deceived by outside appearances; while they have a genuinely fraternal feeling for all mankind and the desire to lighten the load oppressing humanity, their sympathies must be engaged through an exposition of actual necessity.

They are very radical in their opinions, always questioning and departing from accepted standards of belief; sceptical in all matters which cannot be logically demonstrated; reason from a purely intellectual and material point of view; suppress imagination and intui-

Incentive necessary

Humanitarians

Materialistic

43

tion, and always endeavor to explain the supernatural in the most commonplace, matter-of-fact sort of way.

In disposition Aquarius people are gentle and even-tempered, free and affable in manner, and have great regard for the good opinion of others. They are fond of dress and bright colors, always desire to follow the latest fashion and to associate with those high up in the social scale. They have excellent memories, are fine entertainers, and because of their great tact, can adapt themselves readily to any circumstance or environment. They are inclined to worry over the simplest matters, but meet great difficulties with fortitude.

Good memory

They are generally fortunate in dealing with others, are very inquisitive, and as they are fond of study, they make the most of their ability to pick up information from every available source. As all Aquarius people are of a busy turn of mind, they are apt to be restless, and scatter their forces by trying to do too many things at a time. Until they have learned to hold themselves well in check, they are weak and vacillating, controlled by their appetites and desires, and swayed by the advice of their companions. The men born under this sign are known as, " jolly good fellows "; they seldom antagonize personal feel-

Restless

ing, but agree with others for the sake of good
fellowship, although they will hold out stubbornly enough in all important matters. They
spend money freely for personal gratification,
but in all outlays they generally look for a fair
equivalent. They make faithful friends but
bitter enemies, and will meet treachery with
treachery; they hold their own well in an
argument, but when opposed become taunting
and sarcastic.

They have an extremely nervous temperament, and most of their ills arise from disorders of the nervous system. They are active
when thoroughly aroused, but ordinarily their
methods are slow even to procrastination.
They favor literary and scientific pursuits, for
while they are natural traders and buyers, they
lack the determination and shrewdness necessary for great financial schemes.

SHORTCOMINGS

Prompted by their great desire for popularity, Aquarius people fall into the habit of
making impossible promises and engagements;
in such matters more careful consideration will
save much unnecessary worry and loss of vitality. Unless thoroughly aroused by the exi-
gency of the case, they are wavering and
uncertain, "unstable as water," now swayed

Popular

*Nervous
temperament*

Unstable

by the advice and opinions of others, now by the caprice of the moment, in spite of all counsel and opposition.

They think too much of personal appearance, and will go to great lengths to gratify their desire for fine apparel. They are so much controlled by the desire to appear well in the eyes of others that they are frequently

Tendency to exaggerate

untruthful, exaggerating their own importance and that of their friends in their effort to create a favorable impression. They ruin their best efforts by vacillation, and stifle their higher nature by dogmatic materialism, and are, for this reason, seldom able to advance one step in any line of thought where facts are not demonstrable to the senses.

SUGGESTIONS

Aquarius people should strive to strengthen their character by cultivating firmness and consistency in all things, and to remember that nothing is well done without earnestness

Self-reliance

of purpose. Self-confidence is a necessity to the Aquarius man or woman who wishes to succeed in life; while naturally endowed with fine minds and magnificent will power, they are often too indolent and listless to put forth their best efforts, preferring to rely on others even in the simplest matters, and the greater their intellectual culture the more difficult it becomes to awaken their sense of moral responsibility, for they persistently shut their eyes and minds to the ideal and spiritual side of life, and blindly follow the limitations of human intellect. They should cultivate their own strength and gifts instead of aping those of others. We all have our own appointed work to do, and it will avail us but little if we let that work be done by another, even though it were better done. We are here to build up character, and we have no moral right to shift to the shoulders of another, responsibilities sent to us for our instruction and discipline. The world is full of judgment days, and " he who spares himself cannot fail to become contemptible in his own eyes as well as in the eyes of others."

Should not shirk responsibility

Affinities and Marriage

Aquarius people will find their most congenial friends and associates among those born under Leo. The blending of these natures would be most harmonious, and the strength of one would offset the weakness of the other. A union of Aquarius with either Capricorn or Pisces would insure much happiness and fur-

47

ther his or her interests in either the social or business world. There is also a strong and lasting attraction among Aquarius, Gemini, and Libra people.

Suggestions to Parents and Teachers

The children born under this sign are very restless, nervous, and sensitive. They have too great regard for the approbation of others; their overweening desire to please often causes them to misstate facts and gets them into serious trouble. They are easily swayed by those with whom they associate, and are often persuaded to act against their own convictions of right and wrong. A spirit of self-reliance should be cultivated, and they should be encouraged to decide their own questions at a very early age. Especially in the training of Aquarius children, self-control should be substituted for parental control.

Encourage self-depend-ence

These little ones are very loyal to their friends and intend to be faithful to every duty, but their habits of procrastination and breaking promises are very hard to overcome, though as they are easily influenced they can be taught, without much trouble, punctuality and the

48

importance of keeping a promise. Constant scolding and fault finding is very harmful to these nervous children. They should be governed with the utmost firmness and patience, for while restraint is most irksome to them, it is necessary to their health that they should lead quiet, simple lives, and associate with those who have a calm and restful manner. A high, sharp tone of voice, sudden noises, or any disturbing influence affects them almost as keenly as physical pain. They have a modest, retiring manner, good memory, and being fond of asking questions, they succeed in collecting much information.

Govern patiently but firmly

Women

VOCATION

Aquarius women are very faithful and devoted in the home life and to their friends, but when their confidence is abused they are apt to become treacherous and cruel. They are extremely fond of society, public ceremonies and entertainments, and desire always to appear to the best advantage and to dress in the most approved fashion. They are kind-hearted and affable to all, but they prefer to make friends of those who have rank and

Fond of society

49

social prominence. They are fond of all the good things of life, like to entertain, and expect to be entertained.

Graceful

They are bright and witty conversationalists, easy and graceful in manner, sympathetic listeners, and usually win the respect and admiration of others for their common-sense views and quick understanding. They are very industrious, but seldom waste their time on persons or things that may not in some way be useful to them. They have fine, robust figures, great physical endurance, and

Reliable

are thoroughly capable and reliable in whatever they seriously undertake. They frequently take much interest in the leading questions of the day, and when they enlarge their field of usefulness, by trying to better the existing conditions of society, they show great power and ability to mould the opinions of others. They seem impelled by nature to teach in either public or private life. They

Artistic and inventive

make excellent public speakers, writers, musicians, actresses, and social leaders. They have considerable inventive ability, are good buyers, saleswomen, and accountants.

Distinguished women

Some of the well-known women born under this sign are: Susan B. Anthony, Adelina Patti, Hannah More, Mary Mapes Dodge, Annie Jenness Miller, and Anna M. Shaw.

Men

VOCATION

The mental quickness of Aquarius men makes them very apt in any trade or profession. They are well adapted to and are very fond of literary and scientific pursuits. As writers or lawyers they prepare their essays and briefs with much precision, and they have fine taste in the choice of language. In the realm of science and invention, when once an idea has taken firm root, they work with great persistency and concentration of purpose, but ordinarily they prefer pushing the inventions of others to working out their own.

Writers and lawyers

They are natural traders and buyers, always inquiring the price and value of things; fortunate in lending and borrowing, and in real estate speculations. They watch their own interests very closely in all business transactions, instinctively study the character and tastes of others, and usually get their own way, though apparently yielding to the judgment and desires of those with whom they have business dealings. They are inclined to worry over small matters, and unless they are associated with venturesome spirits, are apt to stick to minor trades and pursuits.

Natural traders

As statesmen and politicians they keep fairly

Aquarius

Statesmen

close to public opinion, regard a " public office as a public trust," and rarely ever use their power to oppress others. In matters of reform they are provokingly slow, but when, after carefully considering methods of procedure and feeling sure of their position, Aquarius men resolve on adopting certain measures for the public good, they keep steadily at the work in hand until they have attained practical results. Their minds are

Philanthropists

very active in all humanitarian work, and they like to think and act for others.

As Aquarius people represent the intellectual and scientific spirit of the age, when they deal with psychological subjects they attempt to reduce phenomena to practical demonstration, but when not able to do this, they dismiss the subject as so much rubbish. As clerks they do their work with painstaking precision, and are quiet and unobtrusive in manner; as buyers and sellers for mercantile houses they gain many favors and much attention through their genial personality.

PARTNERSHIPS

In the commercial life, Aquarius should seek a partnership with those born under Capricorn or Sagittarius; as these people are capable of mastering large enterprises and financial plans, they would give greater force and determination to the Aquarius character. In scientific pursuits Aquarius should associate himself with either Pisces or Aries—he could push the inventions of both; his hopeful, enthusiastic nature would encourage Pisces, and his slow methods restrain the impetuosity of Aries. A business association with those of his own sign, Gemini, or Libra would not be to his advantage, because of the restlessness of these people, but association with the Leo type would be pleasant and helpful.

Some of the distinguished men born under Aquarius are: Abraham Lincoln, Peter Cooper, John Ruskin, Charles Dickens, Thomas Edison, Hiram Stevens Maxim, William M. Evarts, Thomas Paine, Henry Irving, John Marshall, Charles Darwin, George Peabody, Leander McCormick, and Li Hung Chang.

Distinguished men

Planetary Influence

MENTAL

Uranus in this sign gives great mental quickness and good judgment, but he frequently works against the successful career of Aquarius people, causing extreme activity in physical movements, too great a strain on the health, endurance, and nervous system, making those born under his influence erratic, changeable, and unreliable.

MORAL

Saturn in this sign has a favorable and steadying influence; he gives more positiveness, caution, and economy, and adds executive and financial ability to the Aquarius character.

PHYSICAL

Persons born under Aquarius usually have robust figures, a ruddy complexion, hair of a reddish brown, expressive eyes, and are generally very handsome; the women especially are very attractive and fine looking.

The diseases are chiefly nervous affections, and it is very necessary that Aquarius people should be surrounded by persons of calm, patient, and cheerful dispositions. They suffer also from rheumatism, gout, indigestion, and many ailments not of a serious nature.

The mystical gem of this sign is the sky-blue sapphire, which is supposed to have a quieting effect on the nerves and give health and happiness when worn by persons born under Aquarius.

PISCES

The Fishes

Planets

♃ ♆

Jupiter Neptune

General Characteristics

Persons born under this sign are the restless searchers for knowledge in all departments of life. They have fine mechanical, scientific, and philosophical minds, are very sure of their facts, logical and positive in their opinions, and while apparently of a yielding and submissive nature, they are really very determined, even obstinate, in carrying out their plans, which they have matured with great care and deliberation. They are precise and orderly, dislike confusion, and object to leaving things in an unfinished condition; they are faithful, reliable, and just in their dealings, seldom look for dishonesty, and generally put too much confidence in the words and promises of friends. They have much self-esteem, but lack self-confidence; this they seek to conceal, and to overcome by being prepared at every point of attack. These people have such strong ideas of justice that, when occupying positions of trust and responsibility, and forced to defend the stand they have taken, all

Searchers for knowledge

Reliable

Tenacious

the bull-dog tenacity in their nature is aroused, and they seldom loosen their grip until they have demonstrated the soundness of their position. This stubbornness in the Pisces character is manifested in the thrusting out of the lower jaw and the look of grim determination in the otherwise placid and sleepy expression of the countenance. These people are fond of the beautiful, have artistic tastes, are chaste in thought, and though not ardent lovers, are

Faithful

very faithful and sincere. They frequently sacrifice their comfort to further the interests of others, and throw themselves with so much earnestness into what they conceive to be their duty that they ofttimes exhaust their not over-abundant vitality. They are impulsive in forming likes and dislikes, and are careless in concealing their aversions.

They are exacting, much given to the habit of self-censure, worrying about their health and money matters, and even when in affluent cir-

Apprehensive

cumstances are continually apprehensive that calamities may overtake them, and that they will become dependent upon others. They

Restless

are restless and fond of travel. Change of scene, air, and much physical exertion they deem absolutely essential to their well-being. What they really require is change of thought and to guard against gloomy forebodings.

Pisces

"The thing I feared has come upon me!" exclaimed much-enduring Job, and Pisces people would do well to take this saying to heart, and profit by it. While there is considerable inventive ability to be found among those born under this sign, these people pay so much attention to detail that they are seldom originators, but seem better pleased to put the finishing touch on the work of others than to carry out their own ideas. They are particularly apt in completing any work which requires great nicety of finish. Pisces people are good moralists, but they lack intuition, demand reasons for everything, and are unable to form accurate conceptions of religious or spiritual subjects. Faith must be built on the firm and enduring foundation of Reason to become an edifice sufficiently large for them to even enter. They consider old foundations worthy of respect, but they always reserve their right to build elsewhere and to reject all material which does not satisfy them as worthy to be used in the building of their own Temple of Knowledge.

Lack intuition

Materialists

SHORTCOMINGS

Pisces people are affable and kind-hearted, but when opposed they become obstinate and disagreeable. They demand reasons for

Obstinate

everything; are very inquisitive and exacting; and spend much time in bemoaning their lack of vitality. Their needless anxiety

Pessimistic about the future makes them pessimistic and penurious. They find it very difficult to change their habits, customs, or beliefs, and this lack of adaptability makes them stick tenaciously to whatever line of life they have mapped out for themselves.

As this sign governs the feet, Pisces people are great pedestrians and natural "globe trotters." When they are not able to gratify their desire for locomotion they become very fussy and fretful and fearful of losing their health. If they lack intellectual aspirations, are apt to become very gross in their thoughts

Indolent and habits—dull and indolent, caring only for their own ease and comfort.

SUGGESTIONS

Don't worry "Don't worry" should be the watchword of this sign, for the mind has a great sustaining effect on the body. Anxiety and dismal forebodings destroy the health and vitality sooner than the most severe toil or mental labor. The constant change of scene which Pisces people fancy so necessary for their health, is absolutely useless, without change of thought; instead of limiting their thoughts to the realm of reason, they should cultivate a higher philosophy than materialism, for intuition often tells us " that all our learning is but a finger-post to that supreme knowledge of truth which is only found and closely guarded within the human heart." Pisces people, if they do not wish to become physical and mental wrecks, must cultivate a more hopeful spirit, and spend less time in thinking of their mental and physical temperature.

Cultivate a higher philosophy

Affinities and Marriage

Pisces men and women have a restless, roving disposition, and demand too much, to be quite satisfactory in the domestic relations. The men become selfishly absorbed in business or intellectual pursuits, and, whatever they may be elsewhere, are not companionable at home; the women indulge in spells of melancholy and fits of weeping, which cast a gloom over the entire household. Persons born under Virgo would satisfy the intellectual requirements of the Pisces nature—a union with either Aquarius or Aries would help Pisces to be more hopeful and cheerful. Much self-discipline is always necessary when Pisces chooses companions among those born under

59

either Libra or Sagittarius. There is also a natural affinity between Pisces people and those born under Cancer or Scorpio.

Suggestions to Parents and Teachers

Children born under this sign are abnormally sensitive, and much of their peculiar obstinacy, when corrected for a fault, comes from a feeling of shame at being detected in a wrong act. They should be taught that quick confession of an error is prompted by the desire to retain one's own self-respect, and is not something to be ashamed of. They are usually good students, but because of their restless, roaming disposition, require to be held strictly to lessons and tasks. They are fond of asking questions, but are heedless of the answers; quick in their likes and dislikes, and so loyal to their friends that they will defend them, whether right or wrong. They are economical, and like to hoard up their pennies; this trait must be very carefully watched, because love of money, coupled with the fear of being dependent on others, may lead to dishonesty and miserliness.

Pisces children take great pains to persuade

Encourage to
confess faults

Hold strictly
to duty

Check
parsimony

themselves that their ways are right and best, but they are very gentle and loving, and can be easily guided by one who will conscientiously study their natural disposition and help them to develop their highest characteristics.

They require much encouragement, to enable them to do that particular work in life which they are best calculated to perform.

Women

VOCATION

Pisces women are very precise and orderly; when they set out to accomplish anything, they work untiringly, until their efforts are rewarded. They have a gloomy, foreboding nature, worry over money matters, and are always expecting misfortune to overtake their loved ones or themselves. While they are much given to the habit of self-censure, they lack self-reliance, and are forever questioning their own acts; when opposed, they become sullen and obstinate, and are utterly unmoved by argument or persuasion. They make excellent housekeepers, with an eye to the ornamental as well as the useful, and insist that every detail of work shall be systematically and carefully done. They are prone to see

Precise
and orderly

Systematic

61

blemishes before beauty, and a fine picture badly framed would not satisfy, nor even appeal, to their sense of the beautiful. As parents or teachers, they are quick to condemn petty faults, and become very fussy and impatient when their rules are not obeyed to the letter. They

Sensitive

are kind-hearted and loving, but so sensitive and exacting, that they look for slights where none are intended, and when on a low plane, intellectually, they are apt to be fitful and hysterical, rendering their own and the lives of others miserable by their foolish imaginings and constant anticipations of coming evil. In the business world, Pisces women are not usually fortunate in their own undertakings, as they lack push and energy, but in the employ

Persistent

of others, they are persistent and conscientious workers. They make fine actresses and elo-

Artistic

cutionists; they have much taste and originality in illustrating stories, and furnishing designs for book-covers and magazines. In writing, their taste inclines to the scientific

Inventive

rather than the imaginative; they have also much mechanical and mathematical ability.

Distinguished women

Among the well-known women born under this sign are: Ellen Terry, Rosa Bonheur, Mrs. Thomas C. Platt, Emma Willard, Isabel Irving, Mrs. Margaret Kendal, and Emily Sartain.

Men

VOCATION

In choosing a trade or profession, persons born under this sign should take great care that the chances for promotion are certain, Pisces people being apt to stick for life in their first venture, because of their inability to adapt themselves readily to changes. They are admirably suited to government employment, as may be instanced by the great number of our presidents born under this sign who have held their positions with dignity and authority.

Chances for promotion

Government employ

These people have a natural ability for the arts and sciences, great aptness in most of the mechanical trades, and a special knack of putting an excellent finish on the work of others, who, having conceived the original idea, cannot bring it to completion. Their perceptions are wide awake where their interests are concerned, and their memory very retentive as to forms and methods.

Arts and sciences

Special aptitude

When the young men of this sign take an interest in higher mathematics and mechanics, they should fit themselves for architecture, building, and construction work. Pisces men make excellent engineers, draughtsmen, analytical chemists, cabinet-makers, account-

Professions

ants, cashiers, and bookkeepers. Many art critics, artists, and writers are born under Pisces. In art, they prefer the placidly beautiful—their writings are characterized by a clear, descriptive style, artistic elegance, and historical accuracy. When there is no opportunity for prolonged educational study, Pisces people succeed well at manual labor in the **Trades** lighter forms of trade. Should they desire much outdoor exertion, they would find congenial occupation in agriculture, floriculture, and stockraising. Their choice of occupation is wide, and generally leads to moderate success in any trade or profession which requires fine finish and attention to detail.

PARTNERSHIPS

Pisces men are usually more successful financially in a partnership than in individual undertakings, because they are rather timorous of launching out in new and untried ventures. An employer of a Pisces man would find it to his advantage to encourage the inventive ability of such employee.

When commerce is the chosen field, a partnership with Capricorn would be very desirable. Pisces is quick in accounting, and his love of detail, retentiveness of form and method, would leave Capricorn free to direct and manage. Association with Aries would intensify the mechanical, literary, and artistic ability of Pisces, and lead to practical results. Aquarius would encourage and push the inventions of Pisces, and show great skill in convincing the public of the great usefulness of their joint work.

Among the many notable men born under this sign are : George Washington, Grover Cleveland, " Buffalo Bill," Voltaire, Schopenhauer, Louis Prang, Albert J. Seligman, George M. Pullman, William Jennings Bryan, William Henry Maxwell, William Steinway, Carl Schurz, and H. O. Armour.

Distinguished men

Planetary Influence

MENTAL

Jupiter in Pisces gives great endurance, persistence, and efficiency. He gives the desire for accuracy, ambition to excel, elegance of verbal expression, and an attractive personality. When the Pisces nature is not so highly endowed intellectually, he gives practical utility and manual dexterity. Neptune in Pisces gives literary taste and love of detail; he also gives love of science, increases the inventive ability, and adds force and activity to the character of those born under this sign. He also gives them love of ocean travel, marine views, and prospers their adventures on water.

MORAL

Persons born under this dual influence have naturally a mild, genial manner, but when opposed become very obstinate. They are chaste in thought, and are platonic in their affections. Jupiter makes the nature noble and magnanimous. Neptune gives a dreamy, listless manner, and a restless, roving disposition.

PHYSICAL

Persons born under this planet usually have large, fleshy faces, are short and thick-set, have brown hair, pale complexion, and light watery eyes. Although persons born under this sign have not strong constitutions, when they take the proper amount of recreation and keep their minds free from foolish imaginings, they usually live to great age. Biliousness, weakness of the digestive organs, pains in the head, feet, and back, are their principal ailments. Plain food and cheerful, healthful thoughts are the remedies for most of their troubles.

The mystical gem of Pisces is the white and glittering chrysolite.

ARIES

The Ram

Planets

Mars   Neptune

General Characteristics

Aries people are the natural head-workers of humanity. They dislike manual labor, and are much better calculated by temperament and choice to lead and direct others than to carry out their own projects.

Head-workers of humanity

To the practical, plodding workers, born under less progressive signs, they are looked upon and condemned as visionary idealists, because, while they can devise new methods for others, they find it very difficult to work by plan or system.   It should be remembered that these people are originators, not organizers, and render untold service to those less venturesome than themselves by suggesting the way and devising new schemes for the benefit of mankind.

Leaders

Originators

In disposition, Aries people are ambitious, impulsive, irritable, and quick tempered—though easily pacified.   In social life they are genial and witty, never at a loss to provide entertainment for others.   They are fond of music and dancing, and always full of life and

Ambitious

Sympathetic

activity. They love order, elegance, and beauty. They are warm-hearted, sympathetic, and hospitable. Their intuition is so keen that it is almost impossible to conceal anything from them; when their sympathy is aroused, they have the rare faculty of speaking the right word at the right time and place. They are very earnest and sincere in their desire to help others, and are so sanguine by temperament that they do not carefully consider ways and means in their proposed reforms and innovations. They are always generous, but yet selfish enough to study their own interests first, and so aggressive that they never quite submit to be governed by others. They have remarkably active brains, retentive memory, fine literary ability, and a very marked faculty of imparting to others knowledge of a general and useful kind. They have their own ideas of right and wrong, and usually prefer them to accepted standards of belief.

Sanguine

Aggressive

SHORTCOMINGS

The most pronounced failing of the undisciplined Aries man or woman is, the inordinate desire to direct the work of others, instead of attending to his or her own. These people are selfish, whimsical, capricious, and quarrel-

Desire to direct the work of others

some, cannot bear to be contradicted or told of their faults; but while they expect others to bridle their tongues, they pride themselves on being outspoken, and the person who has incurred their displeasure seldom escapes a severe tongue lashing. Their passions, however, if hot while they last, are soon over, and then they expect everything to go on just as serenely as before the storm, without any admission from them that they were too hasty or wrong in their judgment; but if they are severe, they are rarely ever unjust. They will die fighting for a friend or a principle, and while they do not easily forgive an enemy, they are not malicious or revengeful.

Quick temper

The women born under this sign destroy their best talents by hasty judgment, quick temper, and jealousy. The men are very impetuous, hate to yield a point in an argument, and frequently lose their finest opportunities by not carefully considering the obstacles they must surmount before engaging in an enterprise.

Jealous

Hasty judgment

SUGGESTIONS

The lesson to be learned by these theorists and idealists, these pioneers of thought, many of whom died martyrs to the cause they espoused, is that of patience and self-control.

Self-control

In their desire to direct and point out the way for others, they should bear in mind the fact that it is better to do one's own duty well than suggest methods for others to follow. Each of us has predilections and ability to do certain kinds of work, and our chief duty lies in attending to that, not in running abroad to look after others nor in trying to reform the world. In looking back at periods of agitation and discontent, we find that harsh endeavors to force results had only the effect of raising a barrier to progress. Reforms come only when we are ready to accept the new for the old. Aries people should restrain their desire to think and act for everybody, learn to respect the individuality of others, to speak temperately, and to maintain silence when they find themselves becoming excited. This method will prevent the loss of much energy, which impairs their health and usefulness.

Attend to your own affairs

Speak temperately

Affinities and Marriage

As Aries people have governing natures, they would be very unwise to choose in marriage those who have also a tendency to rule. A union with either Pisces or Taurus is likely to be harmonious. Libra would be the best mate for Aries, supplying the self-control so lacking in the latter's nature. While there is always a strong bond of sympathy between those born under Aries with Leo or Sagittarius, the nature of all three is so impetuous that there would not be much domestic tranquillity.

Suggestions to Parents and Teachers

Aries children cause a great deal of discomfort and anxiety to those parents and teachers who believe in instant and unquestioning obedience. The individuality of these children should be studied carefully, and they should be dealt with tactfully. They should never be driven nor teased, as they are very excitable and quick-tempered, and so headstrong that force only infuriates them; neither should they be argued with when in a temper, for they are very fond of wordy battles and never admit defeat. The most effectual discipline is to leave them entirely alone, until their excitement subsides ; then reason with them kindly. They are restless, inquisitive, always prying into things, seldom content to let well enough alone, and are destructive, mainly because of the strong constructive element in their nature.

Study individuality

Do not argue

Most effectual discipline

71

Aries

Need praise

They need praise and appreciation; but as they are apt to think too much of themselves and develop into egotists, they should never be encouraged to talk of themselves.

Aries children are naturally studious, and ambitious to stand at the head of their class ; they think quickly—in fact, do everything hurriedly ; their minds seem ever watchful to detect and point out shortcomings and weaknesses in those whose mental activity is not so great as their own. They have very little patience and not an overabundance of physical endurance. They use up so much nervous energy by trying to do too many things at once, that they require a great deal of sleep, which should be taken at regular hours and in large and well-ventilated rooms. They should be allowed to work out their allotted tasks in their own way, thus cultivating their individual originality. A thoughtless parent or teacher usually seeks to repress this singularly high-strung temperament, which is always striving for expression, and an Aries child is frequently made to suffer keenly in body as well as mind by inharmonious surroundings, and by those who govern dogmatically and strive to force the proverbial square child into the round hole.

Require
much sleep

Do not repress

Women

VOCATION

The women born under this sign are capable of holding positions of authority and responsibility, but, as they are very impatient and irritable under restraint, they should be given a thorough understanding of the work to be done, and then left to their own methods.

Irritable under restraint

They make excellent designers, either as milliners or dressmakers; in fact, all artistic occupations seem favorable to the Aries type. They dislike detail work, and when compelled to follow certain routine duties, they always try to vary them as much as possible. They succeed well as matrons of institutions, keepers of restaurants and boarding-houses, but as their manner is aggressive and arbitrary, in dealing with inferiors, they usually have much difficulty in retaining servants.

Dislike detail work

Aggressive

It is difficult at times to reconcile the contradictory traits of the Aries character; while irritable and impatient by nature, they show the greatest self-sacrificing spirit with those they love, and will efface themselves to further the interests of a friend. They are always keenly alive to lost opportunities, and inwardly bemoan their fate. Mentally, Aries women are very wide awake, always longing for new

Original

fields of activity, and are also fond of prosecuting scientific research. Their intellecutal development is sometimes phenomenally great, and as they have the gift of imparting knowledge, they make progressive teachers, but are

Executive better fitted to be heads of departments than class instructors. They are fond of the home life, but prefer outside duties, which give them a wider range of activity; they also prefer the useful to the ornamental, and when leaders in society, they seek to originate new styles, plan novel amusements, and devise new pastimes. The martial quality in the Aries woman's nature is often exhibited in her fondness for chess, whist, and other games, and she is always a formidable and aggressive opponent. In speculations and investments, she is very

Intuitive shrewd and far-sighted, and in such matters should trust to her own intuition. In any work, even in domestic life, Aries women are always devising new schemes and suggesting methods to simplify the labor; and, unhappily, they ofttimes neglect the present duty in their desire to lighten the remote.

Distinguished women The well-known women born under this sign are : Margaret Oliphant, Laura A. Linton, Laura Bannister Chandler, Harriet Prescott Spofford, Louise Chandler Moulton, Fanny Davenport, and Lorenza Haines.

Men

VOCATION

Persons born under Aries are most successful, in business, when they are placed at the head of an undertaking. Their nature is too enterprising for farming, mechanical pursuits, or to fill, satisfactorily, positions where they must submit to the direction of others. They are very ambitious, and when occupying minor positions they soon demonstrate their ability to do better work, and meet with rapid promotion. As clerks they are active and smart, good talkers and sellers, in fact, they are so persistent that a customer rarely escapes them until he has made a purchase. In whatever line of work they are engaged, these people are determined to succeed ; in military or naval warfare they are natural leaders and never refuse a fight ; they are very aggressive, often foolishly so, but they go into a fight to win, and are brave and indifferent to danger. In an executive position or as directors, they rule with much determination and over-ride all opposition ; as bankers, brokers, and speculators, they are successful because of their superior foresight, and their judgment in such matters is safe to follow. When interested in reforms, they are very aggressive and bitter in their attacks upon their

Executive

Salesmen

Bankers and
brokers

opponents, and relentlessly pursue the offenders or systems until they have achieved the desired result. Their minds are very active in the direction of the public good and they are particularly well adapted to build up new educational systems, to explore new fields of action, to exploit new theories, and to brush away the cobwebs of antiquated error from the minds of those who are content to "let well enough alone."

Reformers and promoters

Aries men make good judges, their sense of justice and equity keeps them free from personal prejudice, and as presiding officers, speakers or chairmen, their rulings, while arbitrary, are always sound and to the point. Their writings are characterized by great originality, clearness, and force; as statesmen they are always the enterprising leaders who make a strong fight for party or principle.

Statesmen

PARTNERSHIPS

In the commercial world they have much push and energy. They are always looking forward, are ambitious and venturesome, and should be associated with those who, while appreciating these qualities, will restrain the Aries tendency to leap before looking. Such a union of force would be found in a partnership between Aries and Taurus. The mission of

Aries is to seek opportunities, that of Taurus to seize them ; the rashness and impetuosity of Aries would be held in check by the slow and sure Taurus, whose keen intuition in practical business methods would prove invaluable in pushing inventions, directing the finances, and attending the detail work of their joint interest.

Pisces with his dogged and patient determination to overcome obstacles would be a good partner for the carrying out of the schemes of ambitious Aries. Should Aries and Scorpio or Aries and Capricorn decide to form a partnership—Aries would find himself thwarted at every turn. The tendency of Scorpio to superintend the work of others, and hold them rigidly to duty, would throw Aries into confusion and nullify his best efforts ; while Capricorn, who has the ability to both plan and execute, would insist on having their work done by system—a thing which an Aries person finds impossible to do. Indeed, all Aries people are more successful when they are left to follow their own methods in doing any work.

Among the many distinguished men born under this sign are : Bismarck, Thomas Jefferson, Henry Clay, J. Pierpont Morgan, Rev. Charles Parkhurst, Washington Irving, Thomas B. Reed, and Joseph Pulitzer.

Distinguished men

Planetary Influence

MENTAL

Mars gives the Aries nature an aggressive spirit which is quick in action, prompt in decision, full of energy, courage, and enterprise manifested chiefly in originality of thought, and a desire to engage in pioneer work of all kinds. Persons who come strongly under the influence of Mars are despotic in rule and seek to bend others to their will, but reserve the right to think and act for themselves independently of the opinions of others.

MORAL

Neptune, in Aries, modifies the influence of Mars, and gives the aggressive nature the desire to use its force and energy in the correction of social and political evils, and induces the warlike element to seek conquests in the world of commerce. Neptune always gives the Aries nature a strong impulse to seek fame and distinction in a political or national career.

PHYSICAL

There are two types of persons born under Aries—those who are tall and broad-shouldered, and those who are short; the first type will have ruddy complexion and sandy hair;

the second, dark hair and swarthy complexion. The eyes of all the Aries people are sharp and piercing, with overhanging brows, exhibiting the presence of the keen perceptive ability of those born under this sign.   As Aries people are the head-workers of humanity, nearly every disease which attacks them goes to the head.   They are subject to sick-headaches, mental derangement, fevers, giddiness, stomach and digestive troubles.   They should guard against excitement, the use of stimulants, seek rest, enforce calmness, and adopt regular hours for eating and sleeping.

The Amethyst, when worn by Aries people, is supposed to possess great magnetic power.

TAURUS

The Bull

Planet

♀

Venus

General Characteristics

Persons born under Taurus are natural conquerors, strong, capable, unyielding, and executive.   They have splendid memories, and when studiously inclined are noted for their exactness and persistency in mental efforts. They are affable when not irritated, and generous to a fault, but they prefer to give money rather than to make any sacrifice of time or personal comfort.

Unyielding and executive

Affable

They are controlled by their emotions, influenced by their appetites and passions, and apt to be intemperate, in both eating and drinking.   When they permit themselves to be dominated by their strong animal nature they lack firmness and self-control ; they are slow to anger, but like the symbol of their sign, are violent and furious when aroused. When living on a more intellectual plane Taurus people show great ability to command others and will face difficulties and perils unflinchingly.

Slow to anger

They are usually considered very fickle and

81

unreliable because in their treatment of a friend their manner depends more upon their feeling at the moment than upon their real sentiments, and when angry or excited they **Impulsive** will say the first thing that comes into their minds with utter disregard of consequences or former statements ; however, when their friendship is put to the test and real necessity **Loyal** arises, they are found to be steadfast, loyal, magnanimous, and so abundant is their supply of health and strength that they are able to give practical help without depleting themselves.

They are sanguine over every cause they espouse, but being thoroughly practical, they **Practical** carefully consider " ways and means," reduce theories to practice, and, when they have decided on a plan of action, can be safely relied upon to carry an enterprise through to a successful finish.

Taurus people have a genial personality, are bright and witty, fond of music, dancing, poetry, and art, all out-door sports, and games **Genial** of every kind. They have a sympathetic **personality** manner, and can readily adapt themselves to any circumstance or society; this ability makes them very popular in either social or public life. While these people require assistance from those of more projective minds, and prefer to execute rather than to plan, there is nothing servile in their nature and they never allow themselves to be trampled on by those in power.

SHORTCOMINGS

Weak, amiable natures under this sign, instead of holding out to gain a point, with the stubbornness characteristic of the Taurus type, will resort to subterfuge rather than be defeated, and when they are convicted of this folly they are so abjectly miserable and sorry for their fault that they are usually forgiven and restored to favor.

Artful

They have a passionate nature and are easily misled through sympathy and flattery. Ordinarily they are good-natured, generous to a fault, and have a very winning manner, but when excited or angry they lose all self-control and become very violent in their outbursts of temper. They are extremely self-willed, jealous, exacting, and lovers of their own ease and comfort.

Easily misled

Self-willed

SUGGESTIONS

The influence of Venus in this sign must be overcome by cultivating the reasoning faculties and suppressing the inclination to follow the promptings of impulse, passions, and desires.

Cultivate reason

Excess in eating and drinking must be guarded against and every effort made to learn patience and self-control.

The head-workers of humanity could accomplish but little without assistance from the practical, executive Taurus ; it is he who reduces their fine theories to practice, he who is never satisfied with hearing that such and such a thing might be done, but insists that it shall be put to the test to prove its worth ; it is Taurus who fights and wins almost every battle except that against self.   Should he not, then, strive to uproot the weeds of desire and impulse which choke the growth of reason, and, by expanding his thoughts beyond the gratification of the personal self into something higher and better, become a true conqueror of his own destiny ?

Restrain impulsive nature

Affinities and Marriage

Taurus people will find their most congenial mates under the sign of Scorpio.   Scorpio likes flattery, and Taurus people gain much of their popularity by their simple, unaffected way of making pretty speeches to and about others. Scorpio would meet all the demands of the wayward, passionate nature of Taurus, but steady and strengthen it as well.   The Taurus nature blends well with Virgo, Capricorn, Aries, and Gemini.

Aries and Taurus would not be likely to lead dull, placid lives, on account of the quick temper of one, and the stubbornness of the other, but if both had learned the lesson of self-control, and had agreed to " differ but not to disagree," their union would develop the highest possibilities in the natures of both. Taurus and Gemini would get along very well together, but Gemini would always have a feeling of intellectual superiority which might be irritating to Taurus and lead to discord. Taurus men and women are seldom satisfactory in the domestic relations until they have learned self-control.

Suggestions to Parents and Teachers

As Taurus people are natural servers of others, their position in life depends mainly on education; they memorize with the greatest ease, and care should be taken to cultivate the reflective faculties, or their minds are apt to become simply "wheels of memory."

Encourage reflection

The children born under this sign are generally amiable and kind-hearted, but their temper is very violent, and when excited by opposition they become thoroughly unmanageable. As they are very imitative they should be guarded from evil associates and kept simple in their tastes and desires. They are wilful and very obstinate, and should never be corrected for a fault when their temper is aroused, for they lack moral courage, and if questioned too closely at such times they will seek refuge in falsehood to escape the penalty of their wrong-doing. A wise mother or teacher will refrain from being the cause of adding this sin to a fault already committed.

Guard from evil associates

Never correct when angry

The chief aim of those who have the care of Taurus children should be to teach them self-control instead of rigidly insisting on unquestioning obedience, for if the lesson of self-restraint is not learned and practised in the home circle, these externally governed children, on arriving at the age of maturity, and when no longer under parental control, are apt to launch out into lives of self-gratification which lead to ruin and unhappiness. This is equally true of children born under other signs who are brought up under a system of government which does not teach first and foremost the necessity of learning and practising self-control.

Inculcate self-restraint

Women

VOCATION

The women born under this sign have a warm-hearted, generous, clinging nature. They are always ready to bear the burdens and sorrows of those they love, are lavish in their affections, and unhappy when they are unable to give practical assistance to those who apply to them for comfort and aid. They are excellent housekeepers and do not dislike manual work, but they are more fond of a life of ease and pleasure than of one which calls for great activity.

As mothers or teachers, they govern capriciously: at one moment stern to severity, the next they caress and cajole the delinquent into doing the thing required. They can always win the love of children, but are not so successful in holding their respect. However, their method of governing, faulty as it is, seems just as desirable as the system which seeks to despotically rule and regulate every detail of a child's life, and which makes a yielding nature dull and servile, and antagonizes an independent one.

Taurus women succeed well in lines of trade pertaining to woman's affairs, such as milliners, dressmakers, and seamstresses; they

Warm-hearted

Good housekeepers

Govern capriciously

Professions and occupations are efficient as clerks, cashiers, and book-keepers, and can fill acceptably positions of trust requiring great endurance and executive ability. Many fine writers, poets, and actresses are found under this sign ; they are very orthodox in their views, and seldom depart from beaten tracks.

Distinguished women Among the notable women born under Taurus are : Catharine of Russia, Charlotte Brontë, Dolly Madison, Alice Cary, Mrs. Burton Harrison, Ada Rehan, Mary Mannering, and Mme. Melba.

Men

VOCATION

In making a choice of life work, persons born under this sign should select positions **Executive** where executive ability, and not originality of thought and action, is the chief thing required.

Taurus men have keen intuition in all that pertains to the practical business life ; they are the patient plodding workers who, while not able to originate great plans, can direct **Finance** the work and financial schemes of large corporations, and push the ideas and inventions of others with great persistency and ability.

They are natural students, and are especially adapted for those professions which require great memorizing, such as chemistry and botany ; they are fond of literature and mathematics, and as teachers they are very happy in their method of imparting knowledge to others. Having unusual physical strength and endurance, they can apply themselves with great persistency to the work they have in hand ; in their case the maxim, " Genius is infinite capacity for work," seems particularly applicable.

Students and teachers

When occupying positions of responsibility, Taurus men are slow but sure in their methods; they will wait patiently and with apparent indifference for favorable opportunities, and when they present themselves Taurus men seldom fail to grasp them at the right moment. They insist very strongly upon every personal right, and this characteristic, combined with their power to govern others, often impels them to seek a military career ; when they are in command of forces, and have decided upon a plan of action, they are seldom daunted by obstacles, but march steadily onward to either victory or death. They make but few blunders, their battles are won by nice calculation and executive ability. In an emergency, Taurus men have the rare faculty of knowing what to do next.

Responsible positions

Military

They do not often seek positions of public

Public life

trust or to lead a new enterprise, but when such positions are offered or thrust upon them, they fill them acceptably and with great reserve and dignity. In the legal profession they meet with much success as real estate and patent lawyers and at general office work,

Legal profession

but they are not so successful as advocates ; their first opinion of a case is intuitive, and as they know that reasoning is not one of their strong points, they are usually better pleased and more fortunate in finding the law applicable to the case, and skilfully applying it to fit the facts, than in professional oratory.

Commerce

The commercial and engineering ability of Taurus men often causes them to seek employment along mechanical lines and in the different systems of transportation. When they occupy executive positions they are most fortunately placed, and seldom fail in this capacity to promote the interests of the company. Landscape gardening, floriculture, and

Trades

a great number of artistic trades are suitable occupations for Taurus men. Some musicians

Music

are found under this sign ; as a rule, they are not composers; their talent lies more in directing and executing the compositions of others.

Taurus men are seldom originators or architects, but they are the practical builders in every department of life.

PARTNERSHIPS

In the selection of a partner, Taurus would do well to unite his executive force with the projective ability of Aries or the versatility of Gemini. In a union with Scorpio, the natural superintendent and overseer of others, they should be able to conduct successfully the interests of great co-operative industries. Association with Pisces would call out the practical constructive skill of Taurus along the lines of invention, mechanical and civil engineering.

The distinguished men born under this sign are : Herbert Spencer, Samuel Morse, Anton Seidl, Chauncey M. Depew, General U. S. Grant, John Sherman, Pope Pius IX., George W. Quintard, James Gordon Bennett, Charles H. Cramp, Henry Fairbanks, and William Deering.

Distinguished men

Planetary Influence

MENTAL

Venus in Taurus gives artistic tastes, love of poetry, music, and art ; she specially governs the pleasures of society; persons born under her influence are very fond of a life of gayety and excitement. In this sign she gives executive ability, and a stubborn, unyielding disposition.

MORAL

Venus also gives great love of home and family, but she does not give true moral power to those who come under her sway, and they are always in danger of being led astray by flattery and sentimental nonsense; there does not seem to be any intentional wickedness in the character of such people, their faults spring from a strong animal nature which impels them to lead lives of self-gratification.

PHYSICAL

On the physical plane, Venus gives a genial presence, winning manners, large, expressive eyes, sensual mouths with full red lips, short, thick neck, broad shoulders and a large body. The men born under this planet are usually great favorites with the opposite sex, the women are generally handsome and very fascinating. When living lives of self-gratification, Venus' subjects are apt to have frequent attacks of melancholy which are liable to develop into serious disorders of the brain. When stimulants and opiates are used apoplexy is to be feared; disease of the throat, heart, and stomach are constitutional, but as Venus also endows with strength and endurance, these ailments can be avoided by leading a temperate life.

The talisman of this sign is the Agate, and is supposed to exercise a potent influence on the health and fortune of the wearer.

GEMINI

The Twins

Planet

☿

Mercury

General Characteristics

The principal characteristic of Gemini people is their wonderful versatility. They belong mainly to the realm of art, science, and mechanics, but so varied are their tastes, inclinations, and abilities that they are seldom satisfied with one occupation or pursuit. They have fine intellects, bright, sparkling, and witty, but from their lack of concentration they are not always profound, and frequently have only a superficial knowledge of the matters about which they talk so glibly. They are very active, and so restless and nervous that they are a perpetual source of worry to themselves as well as to others.

The tendency of the Gemini nature is to do two things at once, and also to go to extremes in everything. They know they lack continuity and seldom understand their own wishes or requirements, but while their minds are singularly quick in grasping the thoughts and schemes of others, they seem to require and like advice to help them carry out their

Versatile

Superficial

Lack
continuity

95

own plans and decide questions of importance. Gemini people are, however, just the ones to call on in an emergency ; their minds are

Quick witted

very active and they are quick to take advantage of a sudden turn of affairs ; they can always see both sides of an argument and know how to act in widely different situations from those they occupy. This wonderful adaptability of Gemini people enables them to turn their talents in almost any direction ; they

Inventive

have inventive brains and great skill in the use of their hands; they like to cut and plan, to take a machine apart for the pleasure of putting it together again; to be forever busy at something is a marked peculiarity of

Not methodical

all these people, but they are not methodical or systematic in anything they do, and their best efforts are seldom the result of careful preparation or study. They work at a thing with great and untiring ardor as long as their inspiration lasts, and then will probably leave it in an unfinished condition and engage in a new task or enterprise with just the same amount of enthusiasm.

From their love of change and adaptability, Gemini people are frequently more useful to others than they are to themselves. It seems part of the economy of nature to provide certain types of people who will fit anywhere, and

96

whose radical ideas and lack of method serve to prevent others from falling into ruts.

In manner, they are genial, vivacious, and courteous, but are apt to be inconstant ; they are also very suspicious and rarely ever trust others.

Courteous but inconstant

SHORTCOMINGS

Although there are no more unselfish, self-sacrificing persons in the world than those born under this sign, because of their dual nature, they are usually misunderstood. They are either very selfish or self-sacrificing ; they seldom hesitate to take advantage of one who is hard pressed, and like to drive sharp bargains, but what they earn with one hand they will give away with the other, and rarely, if ever, turn a deaf ear to a friend in distress.

Dual nature

While they are warm-hearted and sympathetic, they are also inconstant and suspicious, and are prone to judge superficially both persons and things ; they are not always truthful, and their greatest folly lies in their tendency to deceive themselves. They know that they possess unusual ability and torment themselves continually for not "sticking to things"; and then, instead of resolutely applying themselves to the work in hand, they cudgel their brains to find reasons to justify their lack of continuity.

Because of this lack of continuity and their

Suspicious

Self-deception

perpetual sighing over lost opportunities, Gemini people frequently become very disagreeable and melancholy in old age.

SUGGESTIONS

Cultivate introspection

The habit of introspection should be cultivated by all Gemini persons. They should strive to understand the complexity of their nature and seek to harmonize its warring elements ; they should control the disposition to leave an unfinished task and rush forward to a new one, by dividing their work systematically, and thus satisfy their love of change and diversity of occupation. These very qualities, if properly controlled, add not only to their own success but also to the success of others who need to have their tiresome methodical ways broken up by the volatile and mercurial temperament of the Gemini people.

Systematic division of time and work

The adaptability of persons born under this sign enables them to co-operate successfully with the conservative as well as the progressive; and who will presume to say that the conservative man, who holds fast to established customs or exploits his one idea, is superior to the wayward, inconsistent, contradictory Gemini, who has the ability to do all things well, and who is just as quickly settled by a responsibility as those born under other signs ?

Affinities and Marriage

When associated with those born under Aquarius or Libra, the friendliest relations usually exist, but all three natures are too changeable and restless to be of much mutual benefit. Taurus would steady and restrain the Gemini impulse to fly off at a tangent, and a union with Cancer would be most desirable to round out the characters of both. A marriage with one born under Sagittarius would give increased love of home and family, and the selfishness of Gemini would be counteracted by the benevolence of Sagittarius. Gemini people are, however, usually fortunate in their choice of companions and happy in the home life.

Suggestions to Parents and Teachers

The children born under this sign cannot be governed by any cut and dried rules. They are so bright, so restless, so eager, that they require in their training, sympathetic appreciation of their complex nature. It is not advisable to keep these restless little mortals too long at any one task, nor should they be per-

Sympathetic appreciation necessary

99

Diversity of occupation

mitted to leave their work unfinished; frequent change of occupation will be found to produce the best results. It is a mistake to scold them for not adhering to a task as persistently as those born under less versatile signs, for Gemini children really require for their well-being constant change of thought, scene, and occupation.

Their mental activity is so great that the confinement of a schoolroom, where children are considered collectively, not individually, is very trying to them, for they require more

Physical exercise

than the usual amount of physical exercise; this fact is very clearly demonstrated by their inability to keep hands and feet still. They are always looking for something to do, somewhere to go, and are often made to suffer cruelly by those in authority, who do not make a study of their special needs and requirements. These children crave knowledge but are impatient of methods; this makes them inquisitive and mischievous. Their imagination is so fer-

Guard against untruthfulness

tile that they are apt to be untruthful. A wise parent or teacher, who listens to their exaggerated account of a simple affair, should not condemn unsparingly this tendency to fabricate, unless it takes a vicious turn, but should mildly disapprove, and direct this trait into its proper channel, that of literary story-telling.

Gemini children appreciate an appeal made to their reason, and will heed advice given in a calm, even tone; but if force is used, and their excitable nature aroused by opposition, they will become tricky, deceitful, and dishonest. In considering the great possibilities of children born under this sign and the responsibility of those who have the guidance of them, one feels that a special training school is needed for mothers. Alas! that so little preparation is considered necessary for those who will some day become parents. And is it not strange, in all this talk of the higher education of women, that our schools and colleges should not include in their curriculum this most important study?

Appeal to reason

Women

VOCATION

Gemini women are wavering and uncertain in their opinions and too impatient of methods to be happy in any but the domestic life. They are natural home-makers, and like to surround themselves with everything that is artistic and beautiful. They are seldom successful wage-earners, because they will spend their money either on personal adornment, to gratify their artistic fancies, or else they will

Domestic tastes

101

give away with the left hand all they have earned with the right.

Sympathetic

They are very affectionate, demonstrative, and thoughtful of the comfort of others, and because of their keen understanding and ready sympathy with children, they make good teachers and fine disciplinarians. They are excellent stenographers, typewriters, clerks, saleswomen, designers, milliners—in fact, they

Occupations

can do almost anything, but their restlessness causes them to seek frequent changes of situation.

Literature and art

As writers or artists they incline to dreamy, imaginative subjects and manifest a sensuous love of beauty ; they are also very practical and intensely patriotic ; they give willingly of their time and money to aid a cause in which they are interested, and count no sacrifice too great that will promote the welfare of home and country.

Gemini women complain much of their lack of time as an excuse for leaving things in an unfinished condition. They like to have several things going at once, and unless they

Success depends upon concentration

have learned to divide their time and work into sections, and thus satisfy their desire for a diversity of occupation, they seldom accomplish anything satisfactorily. They are, however, so versatile in their accomplishments

that they usually meet with success in whatever they seriously undertake.

Among the well-known women born under
this sign are : Harriet Beecher Stowe, Julia
Ward Howe, Harriet Martineau, Rose Hawthorne Lathrop, Margaret Fuller Ossoli, and
Helen Gould.

Distinguished
women

Men

VOCATION

Gemini men being less specific in their desires have a wider range of choice in life-work
than persons born under other signs.   Their
versatility and adaptability render them capable
of filling any position they are called upon to
occupy. They set great value on education ;
and as teachers, lecturers, orators, or statesmen, are noted for their mental capacity and
powers of persuasion.   As artists or writers
their work shows direct inspiration and a lofty
desire to help others through the medium of
pen or brush ; the trend of their thought is
toward the idealistic, poetic, and philosophic.

Adaptable

Poets, artists,
philosophers

In commercial and speculative lines of business, Gemini men meet with much success
until about middle life; then, unless they are
living temperate and well-ordered lives, they
are apt to overestimate their managing ability

and have more irons in the fire than they are able to take care of. As traders and buyers they are very shrewd and inclined to resort to sharp practice ; in speculations the remarkable penetrative quality of their minds makes them very daring, and they are usually found to be on the right side of the market.

Many musicians, sculptors, artists, woodcarvers, engravers, and cabinet-makers are found under this sign—in fact, the whole range of artistic trades is open to them; but as they lack continuity, and are apt to leave work unfinished, they are benefited by association with those who insist on having things done in a systematic and methodical manner. As clerks, salesmen, and bookkeepers, they are very efficient ; they have considerable inventive ability and are very successful in furnishing original designs for any line of work.

PARTNERSHIPS

In choosing a partner to help him carry on his life-work, Gemini should choose one from among those born under Taurus or Cancer. Gemini has the projective mind and Taurus the receptive. Taurus men think and act slowly; Gemini men are just the reverse, and this gives them great command over difficult situations where it is necessary to think

Traders, speculators

Inventive ability

and act quickly. In this partnership, Gemini would be the leading spirit, but his tendency to scatter his forces by having " too many irons in the fire " would be restrained by the methodical ways and common-sense advice of the practical Taurus.

Gemini and Cancer would co-operate equally well, but in this union of forces, Gemini would find himself controlled, and held strictly to the responsibilities assumed, by the cautious and conservative methods of Cancer, who is always fearful of engaging in new enterprises, and slow in making outlays and purchases. Gemini being a plausible talker, is usually able to arouse the perception of his conservative partner and pull him out of the rut of old-time methods.

Association with Libra or Sagittarius would be agreeable as well as profitable. Libra would stimulate the executive force in the Gemini nature and Sagittarius would give commercial impetus and perseverance.

Among the many distinguished men born under this sign may be mentioned : Ralph Waldo Emerson, John Everett Millais, Jay Gould, Sir Edwin Arnold, Sol Smith Russel, Bulwer Lytton, Josef Hoffman, Cornelius Vanderbilt, Joseph Park, George Stephenson, J. Minot Savage, Bishop Henry C. Potter, and William A. Roebling.

Distinguished men

Planetary Influence

MENTAL

Mercury gives to persons born under this sign, sharp, penetrating minds with literary and scientific inclinations. According to one writer on the subject of planetary influence, "There is nothing too hot or too heavy for his ingenuity, nor is there anything too great for his fertile brain to accomplish ; energy, intellect, and impudence constitute the chief characteristics of a purely Mercurial nature." Mercury is always represented with wings on his head and feet, typifying his restless mental and bodily activity, and it is a fact, not a theory, that persons born under his influence have just these characteristics.

MORAL

Some persons born under Mercury seem incapable of reaching a very high moral standard, but as a rule, they are generally respected and make good members of society; they gain much honor as writers and ethical teachers.

PHYSICAL

On the physical plane Mercury gives a tall, well-formed body, dark hair, clear complexion, sharp, piercing eyes, with an alertness of expression peculiar to the Gemini type ; he causes nervous troubles, rheumatism in the arms and shoulders, and pains in the joints.

The talismanic gem of this sign is the beryl or aqua-marine.

CANCER

June 21
to
July 22

Planet

Moon

The Crab

General Characteristics

Persons born under this sign have great love of home and family, and although restless and changeable in disposition, they take much pleasure in the domestic life. They are kind-hearted, sympathetic, and exceedingly sensitive to the mental and physical conditions of others. Their loving nature is their weakness, and because they are so emotional and impressionable they frequently mistake a show of affection for genuine friendship. They have a quiet, placid nature, love ease and comfort and are fond of amusements and a life of social gayety. They are agreeable and pleasant in conversation, and always try to avoid arguments which may lead to wrangling and quarreling.

Emotional

Cancer people are, as a rule, very conservative and cling with great persistency to old customs and usages; they are conventional, and hyper-sensitive to the adverse criticism of " Madam Grundy " ; they love old china, old paintings, curios and antiquities of every sort and kind. In literature they have a great

Conservative

109

Retrospective

fondness for novels and history, and as they have retrospective minds, they like to live in the past, and seem wedded to the belief that in former times people were much better than they are to-day. When they are religiously inclined, Cancer people are apt to be the most stubborn opponents of "higher criticism," and counsel adherence to the strictest orthodox belief. No matter to what party or denomination they belong, they never look with favor upon radical changes; concerning reforms or anything else to which they are opposed, they are very positive in their assertions and maintain their opinions with much dignity and

Dignified and reserved

reserve. They represent the centripetal force in nature and serve as a check on their more progressive neighbors, thus controlling the tendency of others to rush ahead regardless of consequences.

Magnetic

As public speakers, they have great power, earnestness, and magnetism, and are usually successful in influencing the masses ; they are great students, have reflective minds and fine memory, but their best work as orators or public speakers is done under direct inspiration.

They take a lively interest in humanitarian work, but do not like to be hampered or restricted in their methods of carrying on the same, for they have a natural feeling of responsibility and cannot bear to be dictated to, considering themselves thoroughly competent to perform their own duties. They are cautious in their outlays, are discreetly generous, and just in their dealings with others.

Cancer people are fond of travel and moving from place to place ; when this desire cannot be gratified, they manifest their love of variety by making frequent changes in their occupation.

During the day they are bright and active, but become gloomy and restless at night. This is particularly noticeable while the moon is waning ; then their inclination leads them to seek forgetfulness and diversion in excitement of some sort or another. They are so dominated by the influence of the moon that they are often as inconstant as Luna herself, and while very tenacious, they will often give up, for no apparent reason, an object or an enterprise which they have pursued with great zeal.

Both the men and the women of this sign are great respecters of persons, and demand also to have much deference shown to themselves. They have fine taste in dress, are neat and orderly and very fond of bright colors.

Discreetly generous

Restless

Tenacious

Fond of dress

111

SHORTCOMINGS

Cancer people, when not highly developed mentally, usually have a dreamy, listless manner, are governed by impulse and lacking in decision; they are inclined to talk too much of self and family, are parsimonious, covetous, and jealous if others outshine them in dress or station.   They are extremely sensitive, resent personal criticism, and are not noted for their constancy ; but if their life-work or domestic relations are such as will supply the want of the restless, variable Cancer nature, and give the needful amount of excitement, these people are just as devoted and faithful in the home circle as persons born under other signs. Changeableness and tenacity are contradictory traits, but they are plainly exhibited in this type of people.   The influence of the moon, as before stated, makes them restless and fond of change ; the Zodiacal sign, Cancer, gives persistency, obstinacy, and that hold-fast quality which is so characteristic of these persons in all save their personal likes and dislikes.

When living on an intellectual plane, Cancer people are fully conscious of their ability and usually feel that their opinions and conclusions are unassailable and should never be

Self-opinionated

Contradictory traits

controverted ; they are often so dogmatic in an argument that they frequently refuse to even consider the other side of the question, but in social or business life, they display much tact and diplomacy and have so much personal magnetism that they attain their ends without difficulty.

Dogmatic

SUGGESTIONS

As the leaning of persons born under this sign is toward extreme conservatism, they should endeavor to modify this tendency by cultivating more liberal ideas and investigating up-to-date methods. Conservatism acts very well as a check on the heedless ones who never pause to consider, but when carried to extremes, it often proves a stumbling block in the way of progress and reforms.

Cultivate liberal ideas

Cancer people should remember that the symbol of their sign is the crab, whose progress forward seems to result from a backward motion ; they should cultivate a penetrating, go-ahead sort of mind and give up the lazy habit of retrospection.

Eschew retrospection

In religion, they should strive to obtain a spiritual conception of the Deity instead of adhering so strictly to ritualism, form, and ceremony. They should guard against being controlled through their sensations and emotions, because they are natural mediums and easily fall under the hypnotic influence of others.

Affinities and Marriage

There is usually a strong and lasting attraction between persons born under Cancer, Scorpio, and Pisces. The versatile nature of Gemini would satisfy the Cancer desire for change, and a marriage with one of the warm-hearted, sympathetic Leo type, would strengthen the desire for conjugal love. Cancer and Aries seldom agree long at a time, but between Capricorn and Cancer there usually exist the warmest sympathy and unity of purpose.

Suggestions to Parents and Teachers

Sway through their respect for their elders

The crushing-out system is especially bad for Cancer children ; they are very sensitive, and should be treated with great kindness, for while they are exceedingly stubborn, they have great respect for their elders and under proper management become very docile and obedient. Children require not so much governing by their elders as mature counsel which teaches that self-government is the

114

greatest and most important lesson for a child to learn, and a parent or teacher who is fully aware of this fact will study the peculiar tendencies of each character and direct them in the right way.

As these little ones have wonderfully retentive memories and retrospective minds, their story books should be selected with the view to interest them in the affairs of to-day. They love to revel in stories of the past and the days of chivalry, and frequently they have a contempt for anything modern, and really need to be taught that to-day's duties and pleasures are of much more importance than countless yesterday's. To permit the mind to constantly run in channels dug by others, lessens the capacity for original thinking and is unprofitable in the extreme for those who wish to keep pace with the times.

Careful supervision of reading

Cancer children are apt to be listless and indolent and neglect the tasks assigned to them, but when they awake to a sense of their own responsibility, they perform their duties cheerfully and with alacrity. They are very vain, as a rule, and fond of outward display, but as they have a great appreciation for form and color, it would be well to keep them simple in their personal tastes and develop the artistic.

Check vanity

These children are so emotional and their

sympathies so quickly aroused that they are singularly susceptible to psychic influence ; they should lead simple, out-of-door lives, be encouraged to romp and get out of their old-fashioned ways as much as possible.

Encourage exercise

Women

VOCATION

The women born under this sign have a merry disposition, are gay and talkative, delight in all kinds of amusements, public ceremonials, and ostentatious display. They are fickle in their love affairs, but the maternal element in their nature is so strongly developed that they make devoted wives and mothers.

Devoted wives and mothers

They are model housekeepers, neat and orderly, and expect every one else to be the same. They are ashamed of poverty, and inclined to be very parsimonious in their living expenses in order to gratify their fondness for dress and jewels.

Model housekeepers

They have soft, mellow voices and possess much dramatic and musical ability. They are usually good scholars and linguists, fond of intellectual pursuits, are logical writers, and have considerable artistic talent. They are conscientious about giving advice, like to fill positions of responsibility, are active in church

Writers and artists

work, and being very orthodox in their views, seldom depart from the faith of their forefathers.

They succeed well as music teachers, actresses, writers, professional nurses, and doctors. They have unusually sensitive and impressionable natures and are liable to fall under the hypnotic control of others who possess a stronger will than their own. While Cancer women are robust-looking, they have weak constitutions, and should guard against overestimating their powers of endurance.

Professions

Some of the notable women in this sign are : Mme. Janauscheck, Sarah Siddons, Julia Noyes Stickney, Olive Thorne Miller, Kate Sanborn, Frances Folsom Cleveland, and Winnie Davis.

Distinguished women

Men

VOCATION

The men born under Cancer belong mainly to the manufacturing and trading interests of life. They have much mechanical ability and executive force, but they are slow to adopt new methods and are apt to fall into ruts from which it seems almost impossible to extricate them, particularly if they are unfortunately associated with those whose minds have the

Manufacturers

117

same bent as their own. To be most successful in the business world they need to be associated with those who have progressive, projective minds, and who can see the necessity for departing from established usages and precedent, much of which is senseless and cumbersome, and stands in the way of progress.

Tactful traders

In trade, Cancer men are diplomatic, tactful, and active; they like to be consulted in matters of importance, and in any line of work where the responsibility rests upon them they are remarkably efficient. Having unusually good memories and great love of antiquity, they make good historians and archæologists; they are also fond of scientific pursuits and study.

Preachers

They frequently gain much honor through the ministry, and are brilliant and magnetic speakers.

Artists

Many artists also are found under this sign; their paintings are characterized by their great fondness for brilliant colors. They have con-

Writers

siderable literary ability, and in the legal profession, as lawyers or judges, they are great sticklers for precedent. They have a taste for mechanical construction work and like to forward the inventions of others; they are fond

Statesmen

of politics, and show great ability as leaders in managing the interests of their party.

118

PARTNERSHIPS

Cancer men will find their commercial instincts intensified by associating with those born under Capricorn and Aquarius. A partnership formed between Cancer and Gemini should succeed well financially. Gemini has the projective mind necessary in manufacturing interests and active trades, but is apt to be too venturesome, and as Cancer represents the centripetal force in business methods, his way of holding things to a certain prescribed course would restrain and regulate the erratic tendencies of his Gemini partner. Cancer and Leo would work together harmoniously, but in this partnership, Leo would take the lead in all matters of opinion, but permit Cancer to direct the finances and attend to the outlays and purchasing end of the business.

Among the many distinguished men born under this sign may be noted : Joshua Reynolds, Julian Hawthorne, Cardinal Manning, Sir Robert Peel, Bishop William D. Walker, Rev. Henry Ward Beecher, John Wanamaker, Thomas C. Platt, John Jacob Astor (the elder), John H. Cook, P. T. Barnum, Charles T. Yerkes, and the Right Hon. A. J. Balfour.

Distinguished men

Planetary Influence

MENTAL

The moon in this sign governs the reflective faculties, gives much tact and diplomacy, commercial sagacity, mechanical and constructive ability. She causes persons born under her influence to be fond of travel and moving about, unstable in mind, but quiet and well intentioned. If the moon is strong at birth, it is a sign of success and a life of independence. Luna's subjects have many changes of residence and are usually fortunate in their undertakings. She also gives great fondness for speculations and all games of chance, as well as a liking for an easy-going, pleasure-loving existence.

MORAL

In manner, persons born under this influence are placid and emotional; the men are dignified and reserved; the women vivacious and fond of company. When living a life of self-indulgence or giving way to the psychic control of others, mental derangement is to be feared.

PHYSICAL

They have wide but not high foreheads, mild eyes, fair or pale complexions, broad shoulders and medium-sized body—the upper part large in proportion to the lower—small hands and feet.

The ailments are cancers and humors in the breast, dropsy, colic, rheumatic diseases, gastric weakness, and indigestion.

The emerald is the mystical gem of this sign.

LEO

The Lion

Planet

☉

Sun

General Characteristics

Persons born under this sign are naturally jovial in manner, are just and honorable in their dealings with others, and have great contempt for mean and sordid actions. They are liable to go to extremes in everything they do ; they are very kind-hearted, but when wronged or imposed upon, they give way to great rage and sometimes even resort to violence in the heat of passion.

Jovial

When considering the Leo character, one must bear in mind the fact that they are greatly affected by the physical and mental condition of others, and as they have strongly reciprocal natures they will mete out measure for measure ; as a rule, they are not aggressive, but they are very quick to resent an injury.

Reciprocal

The intuition of Leo people is remarkably keen and enables them to enter very sincerely into the feelings and interests of others, and to adapt themselves readily to differing circumstances and people. Their ever-ready sympathy is the usual cause of their being imposed

Sympathetic

upon ; they are controlled by the heart rather than by the head, and frequently get themselves and others into serious trouble for this very reason, but their intentions are always honorable, and they are genuinely sorry for their mistakes. They care but little for traditions and customs which are merely perfunctory, and when an appeal is made to them to right a wrong, they do not hesitate to dispense with red tape whenever they feel the necessity for so doing, and proceed to accomplish the desired result with very little reference to time, place, or precedent, and yet they have, notwithstanding, great respect for law and authority.

Unconventional

These people love the good things of life, and as they are usually fortunate they are able to indulge their love of home comforts. They generally get their own way because of their pleasing personality ; indeed, their magnetism is so marked that they often attain great popularity in public life. They are very impulsive and give lavishly of their affection ; they are also very dependent on the love and sympathy of others. They are active and energetic, but would rather plan than work ; they have a hearty manner which inspires confidence in their ability ; they are ambitious and persevering and have such an imperious nature

Magnetic

Imperious

that they always have a feeling of resentment when commanded by others. In nearly every rank in life Leo people may be found at or very near the front. In the home life they are devoted to the interests of the family and will die fighting for them and their rights.

SHORTCOMINGS

As persons born under this sign are controlled by the heart, not the head, when living on a low plane of thought, their love nature degenerates into unbridled passion, and their fiery temper into ungovernable fury. They are great imitators, and unless they associate with cultured and refined people, they are apt to become coarse and sensual in thought, proud and arbitrary in manner. They jump to conclusions, and are not careful to consider whether these are right or wrong, hence they often form the most violent and unreasonable prejudices against persons and things.

Violent temper

Hasty judgment

SUGGESTIONS

It is always sad to see a royal, commanding nature of the Leo type, degenerate into a haughty, domineering despot. Self-control is the most important lesson for these people to learn, but they seldom do learn it until they have " passed under the rod," and their fiery

Self-control

nature is disciplined by pain and suffering ; then when they have discovered their own faults and weaknesses they are full of compassion for others, and many a sorrow-laden heart is comforted by basking in the warmth of their genial, loving presence.

Self-analysis

Leo people should learn to distinguish between their intuition, which they are prone to believe is infallible, and the desire or prejudice which colors and distorts it ; they should not give unbridled reign to their emotions, but should strive to analyze and control them; they should cease giving hasty judgment, and investigate before they deny, and above all they should try to control the temper which causes half their trouble.

Affinities and Marriage

Persons born under Leo usually find their greatest happiness when united in marriage with one born under Aquarius; both natures are loyal and affectionate and fond of the home life. Happy alliances are made also with Sagittarius, Aries, Cancer, and Virgo. In a union with the latter, the Virgo feeling of intellectual superiority is often aggravating to the warm-hearted, sympathetic Leo; still such a marriage is often beneficial to both, and especially helpful to Leo in restraining his impetuous nature.

Suggestions to Parents and Teachers

No greater mistake can be made in the management of Leo children than to try to control them by harsh methods.   They are so fun-loving that they are constantly getting into mischief, but they are also very warmhearted and sensitive, and require a great deal of sympathy ; when this is withheld, and the combativeness in their nature aroused, they become thoroughly ungovernable and determined to have their own way at all hazards.   They need constant and varied amusement to restrain their mischievous tendencies, and their minds should be kept occupied with simple tasks and duties.   They are not fond of study, but learn very quickly when they apply themselves, and the stimulus they require is love and approbation to make them do their best at home and in the schoolroom.

Sympathy necessary

Keep busy

Praise

A mother or teacher must exhibit no impatience in training Leo children, for they are very impressionable and imitative, and will follow a good or bad example with equal readiness.

Set good example

Because of their abundance of animal spirits

127

and strong passions, they need to be taught very plainly the necessity for self-control, and their individuality should be cultivated by accustoming them to do their own thinking and to decide their own questions at a very early age. In some families this habit is never encouraged as long as the child remains under the parental roof.

One cannot emphasize too strongly the importance of teaching children self-government, and to aid them to become self-reliant instead of depending upon others to decide for them their battles against the lower self. We would be unwise shipbuilders and owners if we set our mariners afloat without permitting them to gain by personal experience some knowledge of steering the craft in which they are to make their voyage on the great ocean of Life.

Instill
self-reliance

Women

VOCATION

Homemakers

The women born under Leo are home-lovers and home-makers ; they are model housekeepers, fine cooks and caterers ; they are genuinely hospitable, but the friend or relative who has injudiciously trespassed on the Leo woman's domains or maternal rights is no longer a welcome visitor. They are warm-hearted and very sympathetic, and when they choose a professional life they make excellent nurses and physicians. Leo women do not often seek employment in the business world, they prefer the domestic life and like to be at the head of their own homes; but they have a variety of inclinations and much adaptability, therefore, they usually succeed in any work in which they are interested.

Nurses and physicians

They have deep, melodious voices, are generous, and sincere in their affections, but are very sensitive, and often misunderstood by those who cannot appreciate their deep love nature. Many actresses of the tragic and emotional type are born under this sign.

Actresses

Some of the well-known women are : Charlotte Cushman, Julia Marlowe, Mary Anderson Navarro, Letitia Langdon, and Mrs. John A. Logan.

Distinguished women

Men

VOCATION

Persons born under this sign are usually successful in their business ventures, and their attractive personality is no small element in their success. They often attain great popularity, and when holding positions of authority

Element of success

and power, their personal influence is frequently stronger than their words, and a favor asked in person is seldom refused. They are unselfish in money matters, but expect to have their own way in matters of opinion, and as they are generous to a fault, even to using up their strength to assist others, they are more successful financially when associated in business with those of a cool, deliberate, reasoning mentality, who will advise discretion, conservation of energy, and less impulsiveness.

Leo people have great respect for intellect; they know quite well that they are often " taken in " when their sympathies are appealed to. They are so independent by nature, that they resent being commanded, and as their **Business instincts** business instincts are very keen, they seem, in spite of the fact that their judgment in important matters is often too hasty, better fitted by nature to rule than to be ruled. When occupying subordinate positions the young men of this sign are indolent and apparently lack ambition, but they meet with rapid promotion because of their pleasing manners. It is only when actual responsibility rests upon them that **Executive** they show their real worth and executive ability.

Mechanical skill These people have considerable mechanical skill, but they are better adapted to mental

130

activity than manual labor, for they never spare themselves when interested in their work, and too much muscular exercise is apt to bring on heart and genital troubles.

Leo men make excellent chemists, biologists, and naturalists. As physicians, they are sympathetic, and their patients become greatly attached to them—their merry, genial manner seems to dispel the gloom of a sick-room, and inspire hope and love of life in all who come under their gentle ministrations. As ministers, actors, orators, and public speakers they sway their audiences, not so much by what they say, as the way they say it, for often their speeches contain nothing specially intellectual or enlightening. The secret of their success lies in their hearty manner, and their magnetic and intuitive qualities, which enable them to get in touch with their audience, arouse their latent sympathy, and move them either to laughter or to tears.

Leo men are fond of grandeur and power, and aspire to lofty positions in the state and government, which they fill in a grave and honorable manner. They make fine lawyers, judges, commanders in either army or navy, bankers, brokers, manufacturers, authors, and artists. All positions of trust and authority are ably filled by Leo men. They are natural

Physicians

Ministers, actors, orators

Rulers and statesmen

Lawyers, bankers, brokers

philanthropists and like to work for the advancement of humanity ; they insist on personal freedom and are always eager to lead others in thought and action ; they are urgent rather than aggressive, conservative rather than radical.

PARTNERSHIPS

In commercial life, a partnership formed between Leo and Cancer would be very desirable. Leo would work with great will and energy, inspire his partner with confidence in his ability, but his reckless waste in expenditures and physical strength would be checked by the more selfish nature of Cancer, who always has a dread of becoming debilitated, and husbands his resources and energies by being prudent in the use of both.

If Leo and Virgo joined forces, the impetuosity and dogmatic will power of Leo would be controlled by the calmer and more analytical methods of Virgo. Aquarius and Leo are natural partners, and their business relations would be highly satisfactory.

Distinguished men

Among the many distinguished men born under Leo are : Napoleon Bonaparte, Franz Joseph of Austria, Archbishop Corrigan, Abram S. Hewitt, Clarence E. Stedman, Benjamin Harrison, Robert Ingersoll, Sir Walter

Scott, Russell Sage, Terence V. Powderly, Roswell P. Flower, Dr. W. J. Holland, and Charles A. Dana.

Planetary Influence

MENTAL

The sun has been given many names to describe his attributes and his influence on human life. As Phoebus Apollo, he signifies the lord of light or life, and his influence on persons born under his special protection is to endow them with splendid health, vigor, courage, pride, and ambition.

MORAL

He gives a commanding nature, sound judgment, generous, magnanimous disposition, and heartiness of manner, which make his subjects natural rulers and leaders of others.

PHYSICAL

Leo people have large, well-proportioned figures, walk with a quick, buoyant step and dignified bearing. They have large heads, full, round foreheads, with the perceptive faculties well developed, gray or blue eyes with quick sight and friendly expression, light hair and eyebrows, complexion fair or ruddy. They should guard against over-exertion and great excitement ; they are fond of athletic sports, and having a fine physique, fancy they can indulge in any amount of physical exercise, and often do not discover their mistake until they have done themselves irreparable injury. The diseases to which they are subject are heart disease, fevers of all kinds, liver, kidney, and spinal complaints.

The mystical gem of this sign is the ruby, and should be worn by Leo people to ward off disease and trouble.

VIRGO

The Virgin

Planet

☿

Mercury

General Characteristics

Persons born under this sign have discriminating, analytical, and practical minds. They
reason from an external and materialistic point
of view, but they also combine intuition to
some extent with their reasoning faculties.
They are not originators in any line of work,
and are generally conservative in their opinions ; they have great aptitude in learning,
wonderful endurance when applying themselves
to any branch of study, and seldom lose hope
or become daunte by failure. They are
self-conscious, but understand themselves
thoroughly, and seldom regard any one as superior to themselves. They always insist upon
being treated with respect, and the surest way
to win a Virgo person's esteem, is to pay
court to his intelligence. They adore personal
freedom, and it is very difficult for them to
submit to the rule of anybody ; when they are
permitted to have their own way they are
peaceable and tolerant of the peculiarities of
others. They are much given to making fine

Analytical

Resolute

Tolerant

distinctions in the choice of words, are extremely critical, are keen observers, good-natured, and well-disposed. They have a fine sense of honor, and never betray a trust reposed in them, but they are very quick to discover disagreeable facts and are not averse to divulging them when they have a point to gain; they sometimes thus seek popularity by exposing the weaknesses of others.

Critical

They have a caustic wit which they veil under a playful manner, and seem to take delight in seeing their victims squirm under their gibes.

Sarcastic

These people have artistic tastes and tendencies; unpleasant surroundings affect them much, even to the extent of destroying appetite and inducing dyspeptic troubles. They love music, order, and beauty, have a fine appreciation of form and color, excellent memory, and love of detail ; they are quick to think and act, are always in motion, wide awake and eager; they have a strong love nature, but great power of self-control. They are fond of home and devoted to family interests, and are very earnest in their desire to contribute to the comfort of their loved ones. They are generously disposed, and take a lively interest in the affairs of their friends. They are lovers of nature, and are natural students of the laws

Alert

of health; are very discriminating in their choice of food, and put much faith in the efficacy of dieting to ward off illness. Though not robust-looking, Virgo people are strong and wiry, and usually live to great age.

Their best remedy for physical ills lies in open-air exercise, of which they are very fond. They worship intellect, and are fine reasoners, but very dogmatic in their opinions; they are also great sticklers for grammatical accuracy and purity of diction, and are difficult to overcome in an argument, because they never forget what they were going to say, lose their self-possession, or feel themselves really defeated.

SHORTCOMINGS

When Virgo people are not intellectually developed, they are very egotistical, and consider their way of thinking and doing, superior to that of every one else. Instead of reasoning clearly and concisely, they are often very "wordy," and talk in a desultory, rambling sort of way, and are not as original as they might be if they paid more attention to ideas and gave less thought to the manner of clothing them.

They are fond of show and ceremony, and to gain a footing in either public or social

Immunity from disease

Dogmatic

Egotistical

Ostentatious

**Nervous
and fussy**

Inquisitive

**Control
planetary
influence**

life these people are sometimes very servile in manner to those whose wealth and station are above theirs. They are extremely nervous and fussy, continually rushing hither and thither in search of excitement, and unless they strive to control this tendency, they are apt to grow shiftless and neglect their most important duties. When they are brought face to face with poverty or disaster, they have so much self-confidence that they are able to pull themselves together without much difficulty, and they make a fresh start with scarcely a feeling of chagrin over their lost opportunities. They are inquisitive, inclined to pry into other people's affairs, and while utterly blind to their own shortcomings, make sharp and ill-natured comments on everything and everybody.

SUGGESTIONS

When persons born under this sign succeed in controlling their ruling planet, which causes them to be restless, changeable, inquisitive, cunning, and deceitful, their mercurial, chameleon-like nature is capable of reaching almost any height ; then they become alert, energetic, intellectual, vivacious, and seem to possess all the qualities which go to make up a singularly bright and ingenious mentality.

To reach this lofty plane, they must make a thorough study of self, analyze their own faults as critically as they do those of others, be as ready to accept suggestions as to give them, care less for money and position, and strive to subdue the feeling of pride which makes them envious and disagreeable.

Analyze self

Subdue pride

Affinities and Marriage

The closest sympathy exists between Virgo, Taurus, and Capricorn people. A marriage with one born under Pisces would satisfy the intellectual nature of Virgo, for to be happy in this relation, conjugal bliss must be founded on something more enduring than sentiment. Leo and Libra people harmonize well with those born under Virgo; their interests would be varied, but mutually helpful.

Suggestions to Parents and Teachers

Virgo children are very affectionate and impulsive, and begin early in life to be " little mothers " to dollies and playmates. They are restless, active, little busy-bodies, and are forever getting into mischief, unless they are given regular tasks and lessons.

Set regular tasks

Virgo

Check unkind
criticism

They are disposed to be very self-willed and domineering in manner, and apt to feel that they know it all. They are very critical, and it is unwise to call their attention to the evils in the world or the faults of their friends. They should be taught that an unkind criticism is often more painful and lasting in its effects than physical injury. Unless this habit of unkind judgment is checked in youth, Virgo people become very disagreeable and sharp-tongued in later years. These little ones are very precise in their speech and the disposition to make fine distinctions in the use of words results in a prim, drawn expression about the mouth, which is particularly noticeable in the women of this sign.

Virgo children are very quick in forming likes or dislikes ; they are notional in their eating, and as they are natural students of the laws of health, they should be given much latitude in their choice of food, and regulated only as to quantity.

They require but little, if any, urging to keep them to lessons or tasks ; they are seldom happy unless they are busy. Their artistic taste and love of music should be carefully cultivated ; in literature, they naturally choose the best. Virgo children should not be allowed to acquire the visiting habit, because of their inquisitive, meddlesome, and gossipy tendencies ; their power of observation and analysis should be turned into its proper channel. Chemistry and botany would be useful studies to gratify their inborn desire to " pick things to pieces.'' Music nearly always proves an unfailing source of delight to them.

Restrain
visiting habit

Useful studies

Women

VOCATION

The women born under this sign have the maternal instinct strongly developed and make the most devoted mothers ; in their love affairs they are fickle and capricious. They have strong wills and seek to control, but if their personal freedom is not interfered with, they are very kind and obliging. They are fine housekeepers, like to have their homes and personal belongings tasty and elegant, and they usually prefer to entertain their friends rather than to be entertained.

Maternal
instinct

Hospitable

They are very sensitive, and when things go wrong with a Virgo woman, she either gives vent to her ill-humor in bitter, sarcastic, but well-rounded speeches, or lapses into moody silence ; she is usually good-humored, and her fault-finding is of the critical, corrective kind, without a trace of ill-feeling.

Virgo

All Virgo women are excitable, and need responsibility of one kind or another to satisfy their restless mental and bodily activity. They have keen intellects, are usually termed " smart," but their qualifications are of a much higher order, and they are really very capable and efficient. They should have, even be they prospective heiresses, a good business education, and practical training in some branch of work or study, as an outlet for their unusual mental activity. They make fine writers, musicians, artists, teachers, book reviewers, art and dramatic critics, dressmakers, and milliners. They can excel in almost anything they undertake because they have great perseverance and physical endurance.

Restless mentality

Professions and occupations

Among the well-known women born under this sign are : Queen Elizabeth, Elizabeth Stuart Phelps, Dr. Mary Putnam Jacobi, Julia Magruder, and Mary E. Lease.

Distinguished women

Men

VOCATION

Men born under this sign are well adapted to either a mercantile or professional life. They are capable of carrying on great enterprises, where they have practical experience to

Mercantile or professional

copy from. They have well-balanced brains, keen, observant, and analytical minds, and as teachers, lecturers, lawyers, and statesmen they have few equals. Their taste for analyzing, combined with their love of detail, form, and color, makes them very able as art, musical, and dramatic critics. Virgo men have very quick sight and equally quick understanding; they are rapid proof-readers, and as newspaper editors they are very successful in pleasing the public; their mental grasp is tenacious and comprehensive, their reasoning direct and logical. As statesmen and politicians they are forceful, audacious, aggressive, and are full of expedients and sophistry to justify their course of action. They never submit to defeat, but they yield to force of circumstances until they have had time to prepare for a renewal of the assault. As writers, Virgo men are unrivalled for the purity of their style, insight into life, manners, and character ; their writings are crammed with wisdom and knowledge of nature's laws, showing well-stored and well-trained minds. They are efficient as clerks, accountants, secretaries, engravers, printers, travelling salesmen, and commission merchants ; in any line of work where quick sight and accuracy of touch are required, they are very valuable. All Virgo people have

Critics

Statesmen

Literary

Occupations

the musical temperament and poetical taste. Many artists and sculptors are found under Virgo.

PARTNERSHIPS

In the mercantile life a partnership formed between Virgo and Leo would bring about splendid results ; Virgo analyzes, Leo synthesizes. Leo is usually satisfied with a general view of things, but Virgo would investigate every detail, know the " whys " and " wherefores," before undertaking a new venture. Leo's imperious will would bend to the intellectual power of Virgo, and they would work together with just the needful friction to keep them from falling into ruts. In a partnership with Virgo and Libra, the great foresight and intuition of Libra would upset the fine calculations of Virgo, and he would be compelled to admit that the off-hand judgment of his partner usually turned out better than his own elaborately constructed theories. Virgo and Pisces would naturally turn their attention to those lines of trade and industry which would call out the practical and mechanical ability of both.

Distinguished men

Among the distinguished men born under this sign are : King Edward VII., Murat Halstead, David B. Hill, Admiral Schley,

Charles Dudley Warner, Ira D. Sankey, Goethe, James J. Hill, William Ziegler, Ed. B. Harper, Dr. Ed. G. Janeway, and Eli Perkins.

Planetary Influence

MENTAL

Mercury, in this sign, gives a witty and ingenious mind, studious and quick to learn, a liking for poetry, music, and mathematics, love of scientific subjects, and good business ability. He also gives great efficiency in any line of work which requires perseverance and a penetrative mind.

MORAL

In the sign of Virgo, Mercury causes much restless activity, an inquisitive turn of mind, love for the opposite sex and for home and family.

PHYSICAL

He produces a tall, compact, well-formed body, fine features, rather thin nose and lips, expressive but cold eyes, black or gray in color, low eyebrows, perceptive faculties well developed, a graceful presence, and pleasing manners. Virgo people have a nervous temperament, and unless they take the proper amount of sleep and rest, are liable to brain disorders, madness, vertigo, and a variety of nervous complaints. They usually talk very rapidly and often stammer in speech. The sign of Virgo rules the bowels and their diseases.

The jasper should be worn by all persons born under this sign.

LIBRA

September 23
to
October 23

The Balance

Planet

♀

Venus

General Characteristics

Persons born under Libra are gifted with great foresight and intuition. They are very susceptible to the influence of others, and will even feel and act like those with whom they are strongly impressed. As actors and actresses they seem to live the parts they portray. They fall easily under the psychic control of others, and they should guard against this weakness by coming to all important decisions when alone ; their first impressions are nearly always correct, and should, at least, be acted upon in the management of their own affairs. They have a modest and unassuming manner and are generally amiable and well disposed, but they are keenly alive to the thoughts and feelings of others, and if they fancy these are unfavorable to them, they become sullen and disagreeable in a moment. In matters of friendship, they prefer the mental and personal qualities, and if these are pleasant to them, they care but little whether they have money or social position. They are so devoted in their friend-

Foresight

Modest and
unassuming

147

ships that a disparaging comment or an indignity offered those they love is regarded almost in the light of a personal insult. They are very hospitable, warm-hearted, and benevolently

Apprehensive inclined, but as they are foolishly apprehensive about the future, they generally feel that it is necessary for them to curb their inclinations, and are often considered extremely parsimonious by those who do not understand this peculiarity in an otherwise generous nature. Libra people are fine reasoners, and have the happy faculty of seeing both sides of a subject; they are naturally given to balancing and com-

Equitable paring, so their judgment is usually equitable, but they reach their conclusions oftener from the standpoint of observation and intuition than from a logical reasoning process. They can plan and devise for their friends, and their advice is safe to follow.

While all Libra people are great imitators, in mechanical matters they are inventors and originators. They are enthusiastic lovers of scientific knowledge, and are always ready to investigate new things. They love excitement, and are apt to act on the spur of the

Persistent moment, but they are both persistent and com-
and competent petent in the performance of their duties. They are fond of order and harmony, and become very melancholy under other conditions.

Libra

They are quick-tempered, and, when angry, their remarks are cutting and right to the point, leaving little doubt as to the real state of their feelings.

Libra people find it very difficult to give reasons; they know they are right but cannot explain why; there is always sure to be inharmony when they are associated with those who demand reasons and explanations for everything. They are unhappy when made to follow beaten tracks or when their intuitional nature is repressed.

Dislike to give reasons

SHORTCOMINGS

The greatest fault of Libra people is their tendency to be swayed by others; they are always seeking advice, wavering and uncertain in their own opinions and actions. They become confused in an argument with one who is calm and confident in manner, and instead of adhering to their first impressions and views of a matter, grow illogical. From their love of a life of sensuous ease and pleasure, they frequently fall into careless and untidy habits, mislay their belongings, and give themselves much unnecessary trouble. They are foolishly wounded by trifles, and are always looking for something to worry about, and make themselves miserable by fancying that

Wavering and uncertain

Untidy

Hypersensitive — neither they nor their efforts are fully appreciated or meet with the proper recognition. From their love of investigating new things they sometimes neglect their best interests and special talents ; they rush hither and thither in search of excitement or new fields to explore, and are frequently likened to the rolling stone which gathers no moss.

SUGGESTIONS

These people must find their own balance before they can attain any permanent happiness or satisfactory progress. They should Trust to intuition — stick to their first impressions in all important matters, as they are generally correct, but they should not neglect to give due respect to the opinions of others nor take a disagreement too closely to heart. That which may be right for them might be wrong for another ; all depends on the point of view, and as the mission of Libra people is to balance and compare, to be merciful as well as just, they must learn to look on both sides of a question.

In their desire for excitement and love of investigation, they neglect, too often, present Systematic arrangement of duties — duties and obligations. If they find this desire uncontrollable, they should endeavor to systematically arrange such duties, cultivate habits of order and neatness, and so gain the time in which they may legitimately gratify their love of a variety of pursuits.

Affinities and Marriage

The sense of personal freedom is so strong in these people that they should never marry unless they are willing to sacrifice some portion of it. A union between Libra and Scorpio would prove harmonious; each would from his great sense of justice respect the rights and individuality of the other. Libra and Virgo are natural home-lovers, and would be very happy together if they had a thorough understanding of their own besetting sins and tried to conquer them. A marriage between Libra and Pisces is not likely to prove a happy one, for the reason that Pisces always demands reasons and Libra cannot or will not give them. Libra people need to exercise the greatest care in their choice of companions; they are quite capable of carrying on their life-work alone, and usually find more happiness in single blessedness than in wedded life.

Suggestions to Parents and Teachers

The children born under Libra are warm-hearted, impulsive, demonstrative, and amiable, but they are also self-willed and obstinate, and cannot be forced into submission. An appeal to their understanding succeeds far better, for when they are reasoned with kindly they will quickly confess a fault and try to make amends; but their strong sense of justice also demands a like admission from parent or teacher who has spoken with more severity than the occasion warranted. They are so susceptible to the influence of others that they are easily led or misled, and so intuitive that they will even act and feel like those they are with; consequently, if they are corrected for a fault in a sharp, impatient tone, their reply is usually made in the same key. The surest way to make these children deceitful is to ridicule their fancies and insist on explanations for everything which seems inconsistent in their behavior. It causes more trouble and thought for the parent or teacher, but is much more helpful to Libra children, if matters are looked at sometimes from their point of view, for these little ones often know that their conclusions are right, but cannot

Best method of discipline

Do not ridicule

tell why they think so. In the moral training of children results are what we are working for, and if our method is faulty, it should be changed unhesitatingly for one which fits the individual case. Libra children are very talkative and inclined to exaggerate, but this tendency comes from an enthusiastic nature and should be mildly checked. They are natural students, and have great mechanical ability, which should be cultivated, as well as their taste for music and art. They are very dependent upon affection, and require much praise and encouragement.

Correct mildly

Women

VOCATION

The women born under this sign love good-natured gossip, but are very kind-hearted, and while they may talk about, they seldom talk against, their friends. They have a gentle, refined manner, and are very amiable and contented when they are permitted to live their own lives and are not dominated by those who demand reasons for everything. They are extremely sensitive to inharmonious surroundings, and their intuition is so strong that they seem to divine at a glance the thoughts and feelings of others; and if these feelings are

Gentle and refined

Sensitive

Libra

unfriendly, their manner changes at once and they become cold and disagreeable.

They are fond of amusements and social gayety, and are very popular with the opposite sex. They make devoted wives and mothers, willingly sacrifice their own health and comfort and cheerfully endure hardships to further the interests of their loved ones. They are always worrying and fretting about the future and anticipating that evil fortune will overtake them; this habit is most unfortunate, for if indulged in frequently, Libra women become peevish and melancholy and exhaust their vitality to such an extent as to bring on nervous troubles, which affect their back and kidneys.

Self-sacrificing

Occupations

Many inspirational actresses, dramatic critics, musicians, and vocalists are born under Libra. As a rule, Libra women prefer domestic to public life; they make excellent teachers of music or mathematics ; they are inventive and original, but stick closely to practical things. They have artistic tastes, and frequently show decided talent for sculpture and painting.

Distinguished women

Some of the well-known women of this sign are : Sarah Bernhardt, Helena Modjeska, Felicia Hemans, Vinnie Ream Hoxie, Emily Huntington Miller, Harriet G. Hosmer, Agnes Booth, and Frances Willard.

Men

VOCATION

Libra men are gifted with unusual foresight and economic caution. There are three distinct types born under this sign: speculators, merchants, and professional men. The first type may be recognized by their large perceptive faculties and sloping foreheads. When these men are, early in life, thrown on their own resources, they soon learn to turn their intuition and quick judgment to practical account; they become daring speculators and stock-brokers, and sometimes, from their intense love of excitement, degenerate into gamblers. The second type, the merchants, are shrewd buyers and sellers and capable of managing large enterprises; they are very successful when dealing in commodities that must be bought and sold quickly; their manner is sharp and decisive, and they spend little time haggling about prices. Experience soon teaches these men that, when they trust to their first decisions or off-hand judgment, they seldom make mistakes or are over-reached in a trade.

The third type of Libra men are natural students and often devote their lives to scientific research. They excel in mathematics and have a strong leaning towards the occult

The three types

Speculators and brokers

Merchants

Scientists

in literature ; in mechanics they are originators and inventors. Libra men do not often attain to prominent political positions except as organizers; their judgment is too impartial for them to strongly advocate the cause of any one party, they can see the good and the evil in both.

Professions

Many inspirational speakers, actors, and musicians are born under this sign. In the legal profession they make able lawyers, but better judges, and, as such, always aim to make their decisions accord with the spirit rather than with the letter of the law.

PARTNERSHIPS

Of all the twelve signs, Libra people are the best fitted to carry on their life-work alone. In forming a partnership great care should be taken. Virgo, unless too intellectual, would yield to Libra's power of foresight and have faith in his judgment. Libra and Scorpio would harmonize fairly well ; the hopefulness and enthusiasm of the Libra nature would counteract Scorpio's habit of procrastination and spur him on to activity. Should Libra be associated in business with an over-cautious individual—Pisces, for instance—who never believes in taking chances, trouble is sure to result, and if Libra is wise he

Libra

will trust to his own foresight and quick judgment and let Pisces seek a partner elsewhere.

Some of the distinguished men born under this sign are : Collis P. Huntington, George Westinghouse, Henry O. Havemeyer, Charles Scribner, Bronson Howard, Theodore Thomas, Dr. William H. Draper, E. H. Gary, and Mark Hanna.

Distinguished men

Planetary Influence

MENTAL

In this sign Venus gives foresight, intuition, and quick judgment, love of music, poetry, and art, mechanical ability, and love of scientific studies. She gives great fondness for amusements and society and love of the opposite sex.

MORAL

She also gives the desire to balance and compare, to be merciful as well as just ; but persons born under her influence often lack true moral courage, and do not live up to the best that is in them.

PHYSICAL

This planet usually gives a tall, well-formed body, fine, clear complexion, brown hair, and blue eyes.

157

Libra

The diseases from which Libra people are liable to suffer are kidney, bladder, and dyspeptic troubles. Overwork and anxiety are apt to induce a weak heart action and nervous prostration.

Libra people should wear diamonds to ward off evil influences.

SCORPIO

The Scorpion

October 23
to
November 22

♂

Mars

General Characteristics

Persons born under this sign have progressive minds which are ever busy with new ideas and inventive thoughts. They are always ready with suggestions for improving social conditions, educational interests, and reforms of all kinds, and seem to feel that their special mission in life is to bring mankind to judgment. In questions of right and wrong they are too apt to consider the act and not the motive, and while their decisions may be just, they are not merciful. They have a positive will, and are rigid to the point of inflexibility; they have fine intuitional powers, possess keen perception, and have much mechanical ability. Scorpio people are difficult to understand, even by their most intimate companions. They are not demonstrative, and seldom show half the affection they feel. In conversation they are kindly, and agreeable enough, but it is not easy to form more than a mere acquaintance with them. They evade direct questions, and their answers, though honest in intent, are

Progressive
minds

Positive

Evasive

159

often equivocal. They express their ideas so guardedly that their statements are not clear and lack force. In the club or social life the Scorpio man is usually a brilliant talker on trifles, going from one extreme to another, in the most erratic and fanciful manner; he delights in drawing out the views of others, forcing them into ridiculous and illogical statements, and the more he succeeds in stinging them into wild fury the livelier he becomes.

Brilliant talkers

Self-satisfaction is a marked characteristic of Scorpio people. They are not tender in their feelings, nor considerate of the feelings of others, and they seem to regret less than most people the loss of a friend.

They have great respect for persons in high places, and for law and authority, but for themselves they claim absolute personal freedom.

Unconventional

They have a fondness for bohemian surroundings, and are unconventional in dress and manners.

Unless they have certain and definite responsibilities, they are apt to lead a life of self-gratification with the take-no-thought-of-the-morrow creed. They are fond of out-door sports, ocean travel, and marine views, and what little ideality they possess usually finds expression in architecture of the magnificent and imposing type, and in music and art.

Athletic

As husbands and wives Scorpio people expect to rule; they are severe and resentful when their temper is aroused, and do not at such times hesitate to show out all the jealousy and anger they have hitherto concealed. Ordinarily they have a silent, dignified manner, are aggressive and executive; possessing unusual will power and self-control, they often gain a wonderful influence over others.

Aggressive

SHORTCOMINGS

Scorpio people usually prevent comments on their personal failings by their reserved and dignified manner, which effectually checks any undue familiarity.

They arrogate to themselves the right to pry into the secret motives and affairs of others, and when they have elicited the information desired they do not hesitate to use it for their own benefit. They often condemn a fault frankly admitted, in a cruel and vindictive manner.

Arrogant

The women of this sign are frequently veritable scorpions, and pride themselves on their sarcastic wit. They are extremely critical and suspicious; every shortcoming, every habit to which man is addicted is denounced as severely as though it were unpardonable sin; their children are found fault with continually, servants

Sarcastic and critical

are watched and suspected, and the household held rigidly to all duties.

Exacting

The men of this sign are not so exacting in small things, but they have a harsh, unfeeling manner when dealing with children and sub-ordinates. As long as their personal freedom or liberty of speech and manner is not inter-fered with, they are agreeable companions, and whatever may be their real feeling, they laugh and joke at the misfortunes of others, and seem joyful that judgment should have over-taken them.

SUGGESTIONS

Temper justice with mercy

When Scorpio people fully realize that their mission in life is that of the judge who calls sinners to the bar of justice, they will know that before they are fitted for this high calling they must cast the beam from their own eye, pluck the sting from their tongues when call-ing attention to a fault, and avoid making the world a harder place for sensitive natures to live in by being more tender, loving, and merciful in their judgments. When the higher nature of Scorpio people is aroused, and they rid themselves of the desire to mer-cilessly criticise everything and everybody, they become a wonderful help to weaker natures; their strong sense of integrity checks

injustice, they dare to do right even with public opinion against them, they champion the
cause of the oppressed, and speak out boldly
and fearlessly whenever their stern sense of
justice prompts such utterance.

Affinities and Marriage

Persons born under this sign are influenced
largely by their passions in love matters, and
usually find greater happiness when united to
those born under Taurus, as the temperament
of the latter responds to their own, and Taurus
people are very submissive when led by the
hand of love. Scorpio people are instinctively
attracted by those born under Capricorn, but
as there is nothing submissive in the Capricorn
nature, there is not likely to be much happiness unless both agree to bear and forbear.
Scorpio, Cancer, and Pisces are mutually attracted, and some happy alliances are made
with those born under Libra and Sagittarius.

Suggestions to Parents and Teachers

The children born under this sign have great
tenacity, and are wilful, almost to obstinacy,
and hard to manage. They are persevering

rather than stubborn, and have a resistless desire to accomplish what they have undertaken, in spite of all opposition. They are made stubborn when they are harshly repressed, but they should be governed with firmness, for, even when very young, they evince a tendency to dominate every one around them. They see the faults much quicker than the virtues of their playmates, and seem to think it praiseworthy in themselves to call attention to the shortcomings of others. They become sullen and resentful when corrected, and will seldom admit themselves to be in the wrong. This trait should be dealt with by an appeal to their sense of justice, and they should be made to see how unfair it is to criticise, and carelessly wound the feelings of others by unkind remarks. The habit of self-examination should be encouraged in all Scorpio children, for they are prone to deceive themselves as to their own faults. There can be no real moral and spiritual growth until they are able to recognize their own imperfections. These children are wiry, restless, energetic, and fond of all out-door sports and games; they have fine memories, are bright and quick students, and should be given a good education to enable them to take their positions among the world's great brain-workers.

Govern firmly

Curb tendency to criticize others

Thorough education

Women

VOCATION

Scorpio women are excellent entertainers, and have an unusual fund of humor, but their wit is generally tinged with sarcasm, and while brilliant, they are not always the most agreeable companions. They are difficult to understand, because their flippant manner, or cold, dignified reserve, conceals their real feelings. They have great taste and tact in the choice of language, and are very courteous and affable. They are good housekeepers, but dislike menial work; they are saving in the family, but spend money freely entertaining their friends.

They are capable and efficient when they have clearly defined duties. They require a strong incentive to overcome their naturally indolent disposition, but when they do take up any line of work, they are wonderfully tenacious and persistent. These women make excellent physicians, dentists, and trained nurses, and have also considerable inventive ability. As teachers they are fine disciplinarians, but are not much in sympathy with their pupils. They rule through fear, and their reprovals are made in a cold, contemptuous manner, which, though effectual at the time, is not lasting, and the pupils of such a teacher,

Witty

Frugal housekeepers

Physicians, nurses, teachers

unless very conscientious, become deceitful and learn to evade her commands.

Scorpio women are better adapted to public than private life. They make fine superintendents of schools or institutions, and when filling such positions, their inherent desire to keep everybody in order and hold them strictly to duty finds its natural and proper outlet.

Literature and art

Having bright and original minds, the women of this sign can adapt themselves to almost any line of work. They make good public speakers, elocutionists, music-teachers, and novelists.

Distinguished women

Some of the well-known women of this sign are Elizabeth Cady Stanton, George Eliot, Belva Lockwood, Jane Hading, Maude Adams, Mrs. Craigie, Julia Rive King, Cornelia M. Dow, and Anna K. Green.

Men

VOCATION

Persons born under this sign have great executive force, and are persistent to stubbornness in carrying out an undertaking. They

Brain-workers

are essentially brain-workers, and like to use their perceptive powers to devise practical methods to ease and lessen the amount of work to be done to the smallest possible expenditure of muscular effort. They have much commercial sagacity, a keen appreciation of values, and great aptitude in managing large estates. They are studiously inclined, have a general fund of information, and excellent legal capacity. As judges their manner is reserved and dignified, they weigh their words carefully, and are usually just in their decisions.

Scorpio men are patriotic. Many brave and daring soldiers are born under this sign, but, as a rule, these people prefer a sedentary life. They excel as surgeons, chemists, and physicians. They are not tender and sympathetic in manner like the Leo physician, but they are remarkably skilful, and have a quiet, impressive manner which inspires confidence.

As critics, political agitators, or reformers, they seem to know just what should be done and how to do it. They stir up the stagnant waters of either social or political impurity, and denounce, in most uncompromising terms, neglected obligations. They ferret out hidden causes, and bring to light many evils which have escaped the observation of less penetrative minds. They sting so severely that the evil-doers feel their day of judgment has indeed come.

Scorpio men are admirably fitted for govern-

Patriots

Surgeons

Reformers

Government positions

Super-intendents

Public speakers, novelists, clergymen, musicians

Dislike manual labor

ment positions. They do not seek to lead or to be pioneers in any line of work, but they like to hold positions of authority and have subordinates carry on the work according to their directions and personal supervision; for this reason they make the best superintendents and overseers in the world. They are fond of making laws, are precise and exacting, and sometimes tyrannical. As public speakers, their skill lies more in sharp, pungent wit than in graceful oratory. As novel writers, Scorpio men excel in the construction of their plots, and their style is clear and forceful; as clergymen they are convincing, because of the practical point of view from which they deduce their arguments, and as musicians their execution is marvellous. Indeed, all Scorpio people show wonderful dexterity in the use of their hands. In selecting life-work they should recognize as weak points in their character the habits of procrastination, the disinclination for manual labor, and their disposition to rule others even when occupying subordinate positions; but when in a position to command the services of others, Scorpio men should seek as employees those who have executive ability, but who are willing to be directed as to methods. These will be found under Pisces, Taurus, and Gemini.

PARTNERSHIPS

In seeking a partner, Scorpio would be much benefited by association with Libra; in all questions of importance Libra would balance and compare while Scorpio would give the final decision. A partnership between Scorpio and Sagittarius would not always prove harmonious, because they would differ as to methods, but with honest recognition of their own weak points they would be mutually helpful. Scorpio is secretive and dislikes to divulge business plans and methods, and is inclined to be lazy. Sagittarius, on the contrary, is an enthusiastic worker, dislikes secretiveness beyond all things, and insists on absolute fairness. The aggressive and persevering energy of both would enable them to reach great heights in the commercial or manufacturing world.

Some well-known men under this sign are: A. T. Stewart, Ferdinand De Lesseps, Theodore Roosevelt, Robert L. Stevenson, Dr. Valentine Mott, Paderewski, William Stephen Rainsford, Amos R. Eno, and J. L. Mott.

Distinguished men

Planetary Influence

MENTAL

Mars in the sign of Scorpio gives courage, endurance, and economic caution; the mental qualities are shrewd and penetrating, and persons born under this influence are generally fortunate in their undertakings. Mars gives great mechanical ability and dexterity in the use of the hands, and when Scorpio men are engaged in work where the favored metals of Mars (iron and steel) are largely used, they are singularly successful.

MORAL

Mars in this sign causes the temper to be furious and violent, gives a stern commanding nature and intense love of justice.

PHYSICAL

Scorpio people are usually of middle stature, thick, well-set body, strong and robust, complexion dark, hair plentiful, usually brown and curling. They have a dignified bearing, and are inclined to corpulency in middle life. Heart disease is the one malady to which these people are constitutionally liable. They frequently suffer from intestinal indigestion and diseases of the groin and bladder.

The topaz is the mystical gem of this sign, and should be worn by persons born under Scorpio.

SAGITTARIUS

The Archer

Planet

♃

Jupiter

General Characteristics

Persons born under this sign are characterized by their executive power and prompt decision, self-control, and the ability to command others where it is necessary to think and act quickly. In disposition they are bold, active, and generous; they are fond of doing good, and can generally be depended upon; they are sympathetic and outspoken, so impulsive and quick-tempered that they will utter the first thing that comes into their mind regardless of the consequences. Their habit of antagonizing others by their plain speaking, and their tendency to represent things exactly as they seem, without considering whether their hasty conclusion is correct or not, is the cause of much of the trouble which befalls these people. They are endowed with the gift of prophecy and intuition to such an extent that they seem to know what is right and best to do when matters of importance arise, and they are seldom mistaken when they follow their inspirations. They are very san-

Executive

Outspoken

Intuitive

173

Sanguine

guine, and go to extremes in everything, and while they are strong physically, they are over-zealous in their work, and use up so much nervous force, in the execution of the project they have on hand at the moment, that they frequently injure their splendid constitutions. When ill health compels them to give up work they become discontented, and are disposed to find fault with everything and everybody.

Refined

They abhor anything that is low, coarse, or sensual, are fond of dress, and like to associate with persons of wit and refinement.

All Sagittarius people have a frank, honest manner, and hate secretiveness in anything. They cannot bear to be opposed, and are very

Combative

combative. Their hasty temper causes them to speak harshly to those nearest and dearest to them, but they do not nurse ill-feelings, and their anger is short-lived. They are faithful and loving in domestic relations; they interest themselves in the poor and needy, and

Benevolent

exert themselves to give substantial relief as well as sympathy.

These people have great mechanical ability, and from their fondness to mend, fix up, and supply defects in the work or inventions of others, they are dubbed " Jack-at-all-trades."

They have considerable literary ability, with a decided leaning towards portraying the strong, vigorous, and humorous side of life. They are fond of art, poetry, and the beautiful in nature, are interested in all sports and games, are fond of music and dancing, and are bright and witty conversationalists.

Athletic

Some of our finest musicians and actors are found under this sign, but, as a rule, Sagittarius people prefer employment which calls into use their physical energy and executive ability.

SHORTCOMINGS

The gift of prophecy and intuition is so marked in Sagittarius people that they have a provoking " I told you so " manner which is very irritating to others. They are too apt to think that their hasty conclusions are always correct, and to pride themselves on being frank and outspoken. Because their own manner is very direct, they make no allowance for those who are naturally secretive. Their surmises are so subtle, their questions so direct, that the person interrogated is either forced to divulge his innermost thoughts or to seek refuge in prevarication. Untruthfulness is to Sagittarius an unpardonable sin, but he seldom realizes that he is frequently to blame for causing others to fall into this error.

Hasty conclusions

These people are too nervous and quick-

Overzealous

Irritable

tempered, too eager in their desire to help others, too zealous in their own work, and unnecessarily irritated when they are interrupted or compelled to change their methods; they fret too much about unfinished tasks, and wear themselves out physically and mentally by their restless activity.

SUGGESTIONS

Discretion in
use of strength

These people should learn, first of all, the importance of self-control and discretion in the use of their strength; they should not give themselves up so completely to one branch of a vocation, because when failure overtakes them, as it may do in middle life, not being able to readily adapt themselves to changes, they become utterly hopeless and despondent. They should overcome the habit of speaking contemptuously of others, pronouncing them lazy and shiftless, and telling them unpleasant truths on the plea that such telling is for their good. The lesson for these people to learn is to recognize their own weaknesses and try to overcome them; they will then be too busy with themselves to point out the faults of others.

Refrain from
unkind
criticism

Sagittarius people have such a warm-hearted, genial manner that they attract many friends, but as they are so often misunderstood, they should have but few intimates. These people never cease to mourn the loss of a friend, and often their grief is so deep and lasting that their health becomes seriously impaired.

Affinities and Marriage

Sagittarius people will find congenial associates among those born under their own sign, and with Leo and Aries; a marriage, however, is not advisable, unless these people have learned to control their quick tempers and their tendency to fly to pieces over trifles.

A matrimonial alliance with Gemini would insure the most lasting happiness, but it would be necessary for both natures to curb their restless activity of mind and body. Scorpio and Capricorn respond to the Sagittarius nature, and the steadying influence of either would be beneficial.

Suggestions to Parents and Teachers

The children born under this sign are like delicate, sensitive plants; they shrink into themselves at a harsh word or cross look. They will work untiringly, perform a dozen little services unasked, and the only reward they care for is a loving word or caress. When they feel that their efforts to please are not appreciated, they grow rebellious and unmanageable, chiefly through disappointment. The fine sensibilities and deep spiritual nature of these little ones are frequently destroyed by the coldness and indifference of thoughtless parents and teachers, who, from fear of spoiling a child, refrain from giving expression to any approbation.

Sagittarius children are very restless and active, and if not kept busy will get into mischief, simply from the desire to do something. They should be allowed a choice of occupation, whenever feasible, and permitted to exercise their natural spirit of self-reliance, as they will choose their lifework much better when not led or forced by others. They are kind and unselfish in their treatment of playmates, and show much fondness for animals. They are very sympathetic, and have a genuine desire to relieve suffering, and are never so happy as when they have something or somebody to " fuss over." They have a very quick temper, and their sharp words are often accompanied by a blow, but their greatest outbursts of fury are quickly subdued by a loving word, and they are always genuinely repentant for their faults.

Open approval when merited

Keep busy

Govern by kindness

Sagittarius children are bright and apt in their studies, and are patient and persevering workers. They are not easily deceived, though they have a trusting and confiding nature. If their confidence in a person is betrayed it can seldom be regained.

Women

VOCATION

The women of this sign are fond of the domestic and social life; they are neat and orderly housekeepers, economical, but never penurious; they are always busy, and have no patience with idlers.

Economical

They are careful and painstaking in their work, whatever it may be, and pay much attention to detail. They do not like to leave anything in an unfinished condition. When compelled to do so they become very irritable. They know how to keep their own secrets, and are too actively engaged in attending to their own duties to be meddlesome or inquisitive in the affairs of others.

Careful and painstaking

They are bright conversationalists, fond of social gayety, and all out-door sports; they are quick-tempered, but never bear malice, although they seldom forget an injury. A well-defined occupation is very necessary to

Industrious

Sagittarius women; they are so industriously inclined that they become fretful and despondent when leading an idle life. They are capable of filling positions of responsibility

Occupations

and directing the work of others. They make excellent accountants, stenographers, typewriters, dressmakers, milliners, musicians, writers, and ethical teachers. They are usually successful when they are dependent on their own efforts to gain a livelihood.

Distinguished women

Some of the well-known women of this sign are Mary C. Livermore, Jennie June Croly, Jane Austin, Frances Hodgson Burnett, Louisa M. Alcott, and Lillian Russell.

Men

VOCATION

The men born under this sign are great

Economists

economists in the use of time and money, but are reckless in the expenditure of physical energy. Too close application to work is their besetting sin. They are usually successful until about middle life; then they often meet with family troubles and misfortunes in business. They have premonitions of impending evil, and usually prepare for their " rainy day."

In conversation Sagittarius men are blunt

and devoid of tact; they are impatient of restraint, hate delays, and are prompt in keeping engagements. They are self-reliant, and
their foresight is so keen that they become
confused and disheartened when they are not
permitted to carry out their own convictions
and methods. They are remarkably quick to
take advantage of opportunities, and frequently
have perfected their arrangements for new ventures, and are up and doing, while other people
are still considering methods and reasoning out
difficulties. Sagittarius men seldom lose their
way even in new and unexplored regions, nor
become flurried under great excitement. These
people are the ones to call upon in an emergency, and their advice is generally safe to
follow. When there is no special need for
activity, they often seem dull, uninteresting,
and even indolent.

They take great interest in public affairs,
are good speakers, but have very little diplomatic skill. They have a strong inclination
to travel, and are seldom satisfied to lead a
humdrum existence. They are fortunate in
investments and real estate speculations, great
lovers of horses and cattle, and are successful
stock-raisers and veterinary surgeons. The
influences dominating the mental and moral
characteristics of men born under this sign all

Prompt and reliable

Mental quickness

Great men of affairs

Ministry and legal professions

Military and naval commanders

seem to tend towards producing great men of affairs. In the ministry and legal profession they rise to great heights, and are beloved and respected.

They make the finest naval and military commanders in the world; their mentality is so prompt, decisive, and correct that even against great odds they are victorious.

Sagittarius men are prosaic and orderly in their business methods, but show their love of beauty and ornamentation by surrounding themselves with works of art and bric-à-brac; they are fond of floriculture and landscape gardening, and meet with much success when they turn their attention to these pursuits; they are also successful dealers in art treasures and curios. Many artists and writers are born under this sign.

Literature and art

PARTNERSHIPS

In commercial life a partnership between Sagittarius and Scorpio would be successful financially, although these two natures would not agree as to methods. Sagittarius would fret and fume at the arbitrary rule, delays, and restraints imposed by his partner; but as the Sagittarius tendency is to jump to conclusions, the deliberations of Scorpio would check rash action.

Between Sagittarius and Capricorn there would exist the utmost good feeling and understanding of each other's motives. They would conduct their business on a solid basis, and no enterprise would be too great for them to undertake. In scientific pursuits Sagittarius should associate with Aries, Leo, or Gemini.

Some of the well-known men born under this sign are Andrew Carnegie, Henry C. Frick, Cornelius Vanderbilt, Richard Croker, Phillips Brooks, Robert Collyer, Alexander Agassiz, Austin Abbott, Mark Twain, General Custer, General Buller, Cyrus Field, James G. Fair, H. B. Claflin, Thomas G. Shearman, and Bishop Littlejohn.

Distinguished men

Planetary Influence

MENTAL

Jupiter is the ruling planet of this sign, and endows his subjects with high mental qualities, unusual discrimination, and keen sense of justice; he gives executive ability in military matters, foresight and sagacity in commercial and manufacturing interests.

MORAL

In disposition, persons born under his influence are quick-tempered, virtuous, honorable, and just.   When they err it is usually on the side of justice.

PHYSICAL

Jupiter gives a tall, well-formed body, high forehead, well-shaped nose, clear, ruddy complexion, hazel eyes, and brown hair.   The diseases he governs are those of the liver and stomach, rheumatism, and weakness of the lungs.

The talismanic gem of this sign is the carbuncle, and is supposed to bring good luck when worn by persons born under Sagittarius.

Final Consideration and Blending of the Twelve Types of People

In the attempt to give an outline of the predominating characteristics of the twelve different types of people, the purpose has been to show how they all differ and yet are equally good. Each type of character is absolutely necessary, and it is the greatest folly to condemn traits of character in others as wrong because they differ from our own.

All types necessary

The duty of each individual is to do his own work well, and to neither revile nor criticise others because their methods are different from his own. For instance, there are certain types who have great executive ability, and can carry on their life-work unaided, because they are able to plan as well as execute, but they cannot work well under the direction of others. Chief among these is Capricorn, who is apt to have a contempt for others whose ability is not so great as his own; but see how cramped his powers would be were there not some who would work willingly under his supervision, attend to details, and leave him free to direct and manage the interests of all concerned.

Capricorn

Final Consideration

Aquarius

While Aquarius people are noted for great mental quickness and inventiveness, their restless, vacillating nature needs steadying by association with Capricorn people, who work by plan and system, or with the Pisces type, who are conscientious workers, and like to perfect the schemes and ideas of others.

Pisces

The artistic and mechanical ability of Pisces needs encouraging. He is always anxious and worried over the affairs of life, and the fusing of the Aquarius or Aries nature with his own gives him the enthusiasm and hopefulness which he lacks.

Aries

With his remarkable quickness of perception to grasp an idea, but not complete it; with his eagerness to rush into a second project, leaving the first unfinished, the flighty, headstrong Aries would not succeed without the painstaking methods of Pisces, who insists on finishing every detail of the work in hand before beginning something else.

Taurus

The methods of Taurus are slow but sure, but he needs assistance from projective minds who will originate ideas and let him perfect them. This want is supplied by both the Aries and Gemini type. Aries is the pioneer of thought, but he would turn the world topsy-turvy in a day were it not for the restraining influence of Taurus and other conservatives, who look before they leap.

We come now to the versatile Gemini, who fits anywhere and everywhere; but he is so progressive and radical in his ideas that he needs the influence of the conservative types to restrain his impetuosity and make the most of his ability.

Gemini

Cancer people believe in holding fast to old customs, and often fall into ruts because of their great distrust of new ideas. The bridge that has always carried them safely over a difficulty is good enough for them, but if the world were made up of this unprogressive type we would never improve, and if it were not for their holdfast qualities we would be in a continual state of change and disorder.

Cancer

Leo people are natural rulers, but their love-nature is their weakness, and needs to be strengthened by a union with less ardent and more intellectual types. Virgo people scatter broadcast their seeds of wisdom, and supply the lack of discriminating judgment in the Leo character, and in the natures of others who are swayed by their emotions; but Virgo people lack intuition, and often find themselves at a loss to know what to do in an emergency, when promptness of action depends upon intuitive knowledge, and not upon

Leo

Virgo

finely reasoned-out plans. Leo and Libra people possess this knowledge, which Virgo finds very useful, although he seldom refrains from making light of it, and has very little respect for any idea which is not demonstrable to his five senses. Libra people of all the twelve types are best calculated to carry on their life-work alone.

Libra

Libra stands for justice and equity. When the people of this sign have learned to balance intuition and reason we shall have an example of human nature made perfect.

Scorpio

People of the Scorpio type represent the overseers and superintendents who demand to be obeyed, and hold others to duty although they may shirk their own. This type is necessary to all great industrial, coöperative movements. They represent the accusing angel of the world, whose duty is to prod the sleeping conscience of others. To do this work faithfully, it is necessary perhaps that they should not be troubled with a conscience of their own, but Sagittarius, who is faithful over all things, restrains their tendency to ride rough-shod over others by demanding that they shall do their own share of the work and practise what they preach.

Sagittarius

Sagittarius people are executive and intuitive. They represent the archer, whose aim

188

is sure, and who seldom fails to hit the mark. Their words strike home, their business instincts are remarkably sure and keen, but too close application to work is their besetting sin, and needs to be offset by association with Scorpio, who is never in a hurry when it comes to doing actual work, or with Capricorn, who plans for a division of labor and systematic execution of the same.